REGENTS RENAISSANCE DRAMA SERIES

General Editor: Cyrus Hoy
Advisory Editor: G. E. Bentley

PHILASTER

BEAUMONT AND FLETCHER

Philaster

Edited by

DORA JEAN ASHE

UNIVERSITY OF NEBRASKA PRESS · LINCOLN

Copyright © 1974 by the University of Nebraska Press
All Rights Reserved
International Standard Book Number: 0–8032–5290–0
Library of Congress Catalog Card Number: 75–127980

Most recent printing shown by first digit below:
1   2   3   4   5   6   7   8   9   10

PR
2429
.A12

MANUFACTURED IN THE UNITED STATES OF AMERICA

Regents Renaissance Drama Series

The purpose of the Regents Renaissance Drama Series is to provide soundly edited texts, in modern spelling, of the more significant plays of the Elizabethan, Jacobean, and Caroline theater. Each text in the series is based on a fresh collation of all sixteenth- and seventeenth-century editions. The textual notes, which appear above the line at the bottom of each page, record all substantive departures from the edition used as the copy-text. Variant substantive readings among sixteenth- and seventeenth-century editions are listed there as well. In cases where two or more of the old editions present widely divergent readings, a list of substantive variants in editions through the seventeenth century is given in an appendix. Editions after 1700 are referred to in the textual notes only when an emendation originating in some one of them is received into the text. Variants of accidentals (spelling, punctuation, capitalization) are not recorded in the notes. Contracted forms of characters' names are silently expanded in speech prefixes and stage directions, and, in the case of speech prefixes, are regularized. Additions to the stage directions of the copy-text are enclosed in brackets. Stage directions such as "within" or "aside" are enclosed in parentheses when they occur in the copy-text.

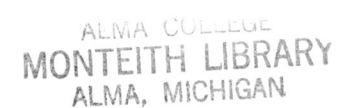

Spelling has been modernized along consciously conservative lines. "Murther" has become "murder," and "burthen," "burden," but within the limits of a modernized text, and with the following exceptions, the linguistic quality of the original has been carefully preserved. The variety of contracted forms (*'em, 'am, 'm, 'um, 'hem*) used in the drama of the period for the pronoun *them* are here regularly given as *'em*, and the alternation between *a'th'* and *o'th'* (for *on* or *of the*) is regularly reproduced as *o'th'*. The copy-text distinction between preterite endings in *-d* and *-ed* is preserved except where the elision of *e* occurs in the penultimate syllable; in such cases, the final syllable is contracted. Thus, where the old editions read "threat'ned," those of the present series read "threaten'd." Where, in the old editions, a contracted preterite in -*y'd* would yield -*i'd* in modern spelling (as in "try'd," "cry'd," "deny'd"), the word in here given in its full form (e.g., "tried," "cried," "denied").

Punctuation has been brought into accord with modern practices. The effort here has been to achieve a balance between the generally light pointing of the old editions, and a system of punctuation which, without overloading the text with exclamation marks, semicolons, and dashes, will make the often loosely flowing verse (and prose) of the original syntactically intelligible to the modern reader. Dashes are regularly used only to indicate interrupted speeches, or shifts of address within a single speech.

Explanatory notes, chiefly concerned with glossing obsolete words and phrases, are printed below the textual notes at the bottom of each page. References to stage directions in the notes follow the admirable system of the Revels editions, whereby stage directions are keyed, decimally, to the line of the text before or after which they occur. Thus, a note on 0.2 has reference to the second line of the stage direction at the beginning of the scene in question. A note on 115.1 has reference to the first line of the stage direction following line 115 of the text of the relevant scene.

CYRUS HOY

University of Rochester

Contents

Regents Renaissance Drama Series   v
List of Abbreviations   ix
Introduction   xi

PHILASTER   5
Appendix A: The Beginning and Ending of the Q1 Text   121
Appendix B: Principal Substantive Variants in Early Texts   134
Appendix C: Chronology   142

List of Abbreviations

Boas	Frederick S. Boas, ed. *Philaster*. London, 1898.
Daniel	P. A. Daniel, ed. *Philaster*, in *The Works of Francis Beaumont and John Fletcher*, Variorum Edition, Vol. I. London, 1904.
Dyce	Alexander Dyce, ed. *Philaster*, in *The Works of Beaumont and Fletcher*, Vol. I. London, 1843.
ex. n.	explanatory notes
F	The second folio edition of the plays in the Beaumont and Fletcher canon, published in 1679 and including *Philaster* (as the first folio of 1647 had not)
Mason	John Monck Mason. *Comments on the Plays of Beaumont and Fletcher, with an Appendix, containing some further Observations on Shakespeare*. London, 1797.
OED	*Oxford English Dictionary*
om.	omitted
Onions	C. T. Onions. *A Shakespeare Glossary*. Oxford, 1911.
Q1	The earliest text of *Philaster*, a quarto of 1620
Q2	The second quarto, 1622, used as copy-text by all modern editors
Q3	The third quarto, 1628
Q4	The fourth quarto, 1634
Q5	The fifth quarto, 1639
Q6	The sixth quarto, 1652
Q7	The seventh quarto, around 1661
Q8	The eighth quarto, after 1661
Q9	The ninth quarto, 1687, postdating the second folio edition of *Philaster* in 1679
S.D.	stage direction
S.P.	speech prefix

LIST OF ABBREVIATIONS

Theobald L. Theobald, T. Seward, and J. Sympson, eds. *The Works of Beaumont and Fletcher.* 10 vols. London, 1750. *Philaster,* in Vol. I.

Turner Robert K. Turner, ed. *Philaster,* in *The Dramatic Works in the Beaumont and Fletcher Canon,* Vol. I. Cambridge, 1966.

uncorr. uncorrected

Weber Henry Weber, ed. *Philaster,* in *The Works of Beaumont and Fletcher,* Vol. I. Edinburgh, 1812.

Introduction

Philaster is the first of the famous tragicomedies written by Francis Beaumont and John Fletcher during their relatively brief period of collaboration, from approximately 1607–8 until Beaumont's retirement in 1613. Each had written commercially unsuccessful plays before the collaboration began—Beaumont the satiric *Knight of the Burning Pestle* and Fletcher the pastoral *Faithful Shepherdess*—and Fletcher continued his career as chief playwright for Shakespeare's old company, the King's Men, singly and in collaboration with such writers as Philip Massinger, until his death in 1625. *Philaster* was written around 1608–10.[1] Beaumont composed by far the larger portion of the play,[2] but the

---

[1] There may be a reference to *Philaster* under its subtitle "Love Lies a-Bleeding" in an epigram by John Davies in *The Scourge of Folly*, entered in the Stationers' Register in October, 1610. Charles Mills Gayley (*Beaumont the Dramatist* [New York, 1914], p. 105) believes that *Philaster* was first acted by the King's Men sometime between December 7, 1609, and July 12, 1610, when brief respites from the plague permitted theatrical performances. Evidence of a later date is presented by J. E. Savage in "The 'Gaping Wounds' in the Text of *Philaster*," *Philological Quarterly*, XXVIII (1949), 443–457: references to a platform which Pharamond is reported going to see at V.iii.3 may suggest a platform on which James I heard and dismissed charges of inefficiency against the navy on May 8, 1609; and the subsequent launching of a ship named the Prince Royal on September 24, 1610, may be referred to at V.iv.19–20. Peter Davison in "The Serious Concerns of *Philaster*," *ELH*, XXX (1963), 1–15, believes that certain passages in the play may reflect actual phrases in King James's speech to Parliament on March 21, 1610. Marco Mincoff ("*The Faithful Shepherdess:* A Fletcherian Experiment," *Renaissance Drama*, IX [1966], 163–177) suggests a much earlier date for *Philaster*, ca. 1607, chiefly because he sees a line of development in the jealous-lover, wounded-lady motif from *Othello* to *Philaster* to *The Faithful Shepherdess*. He also suspects stage performance before the use of the Blackfriars Theatre by the King's Men and before plague-induced interruptions of performances in 1608–9.

[2] Cyrus Hoy in "The Shares of Fletcher and His Collaborators in the Beaumont and Fletcher Canon (III)," *Studies in Bibliography*,

INTRODUCTION

many similarities between *Philaster* and his earlier play *The Faithful Shepherdess* suggest that Fletcher led the way in planning the tragicomic direction which the new play took. An immediate success, *Philaster* was acted by the King's Men at both the Globe and Blackfriars theaters and at court in 1612–13. It appeared in nine quarto editions during the seventeenth century, beginning with the mangled text of the 1620 edition which was quickly superseded by the "good" text of the 1622 quarto and its seven subsequent reprints, and in the second folio of Beaumont and Fletcher's works in 1679; its popularity continued through the Restoration period in such adaptations as Buckingham's *The Restauration* and Elkanah Settle's *Philaster*.[3]

Philaster is an especially fascinating play for the modern reader because it combines a well-managed plot, volatile characters, and excellent poetic dialogue with an amazingly complex wealth of literary traditions and Jacobean attitudes. It is a difficult play to approach, however, like all the writings of the two gentlemen-collaborators, because the vantage point from which a Beaumont and Fletcher play is viewed makes a great difference in the critical appraisal arrived at;[4] yet there is no agreement among critics on the best vantage point to choose. The nineteenth-century

---

XI (1958), believes that "Beaumont's is the controlling hand" (p. 95) and lists these scenes for the two playwrights: for Beaumont, I, 2; II, 1, 3, 4a (to Pharamond's entrance); III; IV, 3–6; V, 1–2, 3a (to king's exit), 5; for Fletcher, I, 1; II, 2, 4b (from Pharamond's entrance to end); IV, 1–2; V, 3b (from king's exit to end), 4. E. H. C. Oliphant in *The Plays of Beaumont and Fletcher: An Attempt to Determine Their Respective Shares and the Shares of Others* (New Haven, 1927) assigns Fletcher (p. 204) only I, 1b (from the beginning of Pharamond's speech); II, 4b (after Megra's entrance); and V, 3–4. However, he lists the latter parts of the second scenes of both II and III as having been written jointly by Beaumont and Fletcher.

[3] P. A. Daniel, editor of *Philaster* for the Variorum Edition of *The Works of Beaumont and Fletcher*, vol. I (London, 1904), lists most of the significant dates in his introduction, pp. 116–121. A. C. Sprague's *Beaumont and Fletcher on the Restoration Stage* (Cambridge, Mass., 1926) discusses adaptations of *Philaster*.

[4] Robert Ornstein has commented that plays like *Philaster* and *The Maid's Tragedy* are "constructed in the manner of optical illusions. They quite literally change shape when viewed from different perspectives and distances" (*The Moral Vision of Jacobean Tragedy* [Madison, Wisc., 1960], p. 179).

INTRODUCTION

predilection, seen especially in Coleridge, Lamb, and Swinburne, for approaching Beaumont and Fletcher plays from the standpoint of Shakespearean drama has continued to some extent into the twentieth century, leading to the familiar charges of opportunism, sensationalism, and decadence. A more popular recent vantage point for critics has been the Jacobean world of tension and change, the "all coherence gone" world of John Donne which also prefigures the Cavalier world with its loss of such comfortable concepts as that of the benevolent, all-powerful king. *Philaster* has indeed many connections with the Elizabethan and Jacobean worlds, but it also has significant connections with the worlds of such diverse figures as Theocritus and Ovid, Seneca the Elder, Guarini, and Montemayor. It may never again be a popular play (typically, critics disagree on the possible reactions of a modern audience to *Philaster*), but it is a play well worth the study necessary to understand it.

Plot and characterization in *Philaster* are fairly typical of the tragicomic romance developed by Beaumont and Fletcher. The hero is a noble, generous, chivalrous young prince of Sicily who suffers from a Hamlet-like derangement because his father has been overthrown and presumably killed in wars with "the late king of Calabria." The present king, whose daughter Arethusa is Philaster's love, holds the thrones of both Sicily and Calabria, yet experiences pangs of conscience reminiscent of Henry IV and Claudius over his unrightful seizure of power belonging to Philaster. He has betrothed his only child Arethusa to the Spanish prince Pharamond, a lustful braggart, to strengthen his hold on the two thrones and hopefully to counteract Philaster's great popularity with the Sicilian people. The principal plot complication is introduced when Pharamond's liaison with a lady of the court named Megra is discovered and, to save herself, she falsely accuses Arethusa of a love affair with the page-boy Bellario. Philaster believes the accusation because a trusted courtier, Dion, wishing to force Philaster into open insurrection against the king, swears to the young prince that he personally knows the charge to be true.

Philaster's Hamlet-like melancholy turns now to Othello-like jealousy and a desire to punish the supposed evil of Arethusa. Act IV brings all the characters into a woods near the palace;

Introduction

the courtiers have come to hunt whereas Philaster, Arethusa, and Bellario are disconsolately wandering. In an action which one critic has called "the most astonishing lapse in any hero of Jacobean romance,"[5] Philaster wounds both Bellario and Arethusa and then hides to escape his pursuers. He regains his tattered nobility when he "creeps out of a bush" to admit his guilt in the wounding of Arethusa in order to save Bellario from false blame for the deed. Arethusa gains custody of the two prisoners, Bellario and Philaster. A three-way reconciliation occurs, and Arethusa and Philaster are married in prison.

The surprise ending, which was soon to become a hallmark of Beaumont and Fletcher's work, is initiated when the king accepts Philaster as his son-in-law and heir but is forced by Megra to move against Bellario on the charge of illicit love-making with Arethusa. Threatened with stripping and torture, Bellario reluctantly reveals that "he" is Dion's daughter Euphrasia, supposedly on a pilgrimage but actually at court because of a hopeless love for Philaster. Thus Dion is forced to realize that he has harmed his own daughter by pressing charges against Bellario which he knew to be untrue. His stratagem has in fact led to a citizens' uprising against the king, brought on by reports of Philaster's imprisonment, which Philaster has easily quelled by news of his own reconciliation with the king. All ends happily with the lovers married, the citizens quieted, Pharamond and Megra expelled from court, and Euphrasia accepted into the household of Philaster and Arethusa. The king sums up a moral of sorts in the final lines of the play:

> Let princes learn
> By this to rule the passions of their blood;
> For what heaven wills can never be withstood.

It is a play that would almost certainly be more effective when competently acted on stage than when read, but performances of Beaumont and Fletcher plays virtually ceased with the Restoration. There is strength in the conversational, vigorous, yet lyrical blank verse which is often missed in reading *Philaster*.

---

[5] Harold S. Wilson, "*Philaster* and *Cymbeline*," *English Institute Essays* (1951), p. 159.

INTRODUCTION

The plot is an eminently actable one, varying from forthright scenes between the wicked lovers Pharamond and Megra to hectic man-in-the-street scenes with the rebellious apprentices and shopkeepers to scenes of pastoral lyricism involving the pensive page Bellario-Euphrasia. The blending of pastoral romance with the political themes of civil insurrection and unrightful rule is accomplished skillfully without the sensationalism and occasional salaciousness of some later Beaumont and Fletcher plays and also without the obvious mocking of the pastoral world by the courtly (and vice versa) found in a play like Shakespeare's *As You Like It*. Either in reading the play or seeing it acted, a sensitive observer is likely to react initially as Swinburne did when he called *Philaster* "the loveliest though not the loftiest of tragic plays which we owe to the comrades or the successors of Shakespeare."[6] Yet it is a far more complex play than such a reaction might indicate. There is no better way to sense this rich complexity than to trace some of the many influences on *Philaster*.

First, there are the two Sicilies which are blended in the pastoral-political plot of *Philaster*. As Eugene Waith has pointed out, "The spectacular history of Sicily was recent enough to be well known in the early seventeenth century"; and the events in *Philaster*, while not reflecting any specific situation, are close enough to actuality to suggest some reliance on real events in Sicily: several Sicilian kings had been dukes of Calabria, they frequently sought support of a foreign alliance, and their thrones were often seized by force.[7] Beaumont and Fletcher probably exploited resemblances between Sicily and the England of James I, such as *Philaster*'s king being a monarch of two recently joined kingdoms who desired closer ties with Spain. But there is also the Sicily of Theocritus,[8] the pastoral poet of the third century B.C., who may have been a native of Syracuse where the sacred fountain Arethusa was located. Beaumont and

---

[6] "Beaumont and Fletcher," in *The Complete Works of Algernon Charles Swinburne*, ed. Edmund Gosse and T. J. Wise, XII (*Prose Works*, II [New York, 1926]), 413.

[7] Waith, *The Pattern of Tragicomedy in Beaumont and Fletcher* (New Haven, 1952), p. 15.

[8] Ibid., p. 16.

INTRODUCTION

Fletcher would have known Ovid's account of the miraculous forming of this fountain in the *Metamorphoses*, where the sea nymph Arethusa tells Ceres of her escape from the lustful river god Alpheus through the intervention of Artemis (Diana). The goddess turns Arethusa into an underground stream which disappears from Elis, on the Greek Peloponnesus, and reappears as a fountain on Ortygia, an island on which part of the city of Syracuse was built. Later tradition, alluded to by Ovid in the *Amores*, permits Alpheus to pursue Arethusa and to mingle his waters with hers; the second century B.C. Syracusan poet Moschus mentions flowers that Alpheus causes to appear in the fountain as gifts to Arethusa.[9] Ovid credits Arethusa with saving Sicily from famine and pestilence visited upon the country by Ceres's curse.[10] And the fact that arethusa is the name of a bog orchid, as love-lies-ableeding (*Philaster*'s subtitle) is the name of a purplish garden plant, adds to the pastoral connotations of the name. Theocritus and Ovid both tell the story of another sea divinity, the Nereid Galatea, who mocks the hopeless love of Polyphemus, the Cyclops,[11] much as Galatea in *Philaster* scorns Pharamond's overtures to her. Beaumont and Fletcher's audience, with its large contingent of young, classically educated Jacobean gentlemen, would have derived appreciative enjoyment from this unusual blending of pastoral myths with Sicilian "pseudohistory," as Waith calls it, and contemporary English politics.

The basic world of *Philaster* is that of the pastoral romance, especially well known to Elizabethans in two vastly influential works, Montemayor's *Diana*, including the continuation by Alonso Perez, and Sidney's *Arcadia*. The plots of both *Diana* and the

[9] *Metamorphoses* v.572–641. Edith Hamilton retells the myths of Arethusa in her *Mythology* (Mentor Books [New York, 1940]), p. 116. See also Wilmon Brewer, *Ovid's "Metamorphoses" in European Culture*, Books I–V (Boston, 1933), p. 206. The myth of Arethusa's fountain may have influenced Philaster's description of the discovery of Bellario beside a fountain with a garland of flowers (I.ii.113–142).

[10] *Metamorphoses* v.487–508. See Charles Mills Gayley, *The Classic Myths in English Literature* (Boston, 1893), p. 183.

[11] Hamilton, *Mythology*, pp. 84–85; Gayley, *Classic Myths*, pp. 215–217. The story is found in Theocritus, Idyl VI and Idyl XI, and in *Metamorphoses* xiii.750–897.

INTRODUCTION

Arcadia contain characters and events much like those in *Philaster*: noble young princes beset by evil tyrants and bragging poltroons but loved by gentle ladies and aided by lovelorn girls disguised as pages.[12] Philaster's name may be an adaptation of Astrophel's, the star-lover of Sidney's sonnet sequence *Astrophel and Stella*.[13] Sidney employs this sort of anagram when in the old *Arcadia* a Philaster prototype, noble young prince Pyrocles, disguises himself as an Amazon named Cleophila to be near his love, princess Philoclea. As T. P. Harrison comments, the distant settings, improbable situations, unnatural characters, and sentimental atmosphere found in plays like *Philaster* could have been drawn from countless romantic tales by Spanish writers like Cervantes, Lope de Vega, Gonzalo de Cespedes, and Mateo Aleman,[14] as well as from Montemayor and Sidney. Shakespeare probably used similar sources for such plays as *The Two Gentlemen of Verona* and *Twelfth Night*.

The play most nearly prefiguring *Philaster* in its pastoral aspects is Fletcher's own *The Faithful Shepherdess*, written about 1608.[15] W. W. Greg, in *Pastoral Poetry and Pastoral Drama*,

[12] T. P. Harrison, Jr., traces similarities between *Philaster* and Alonso Perez's continuation of *Diana* in "A Probable Source of Beaumont and Fletcher's *Philaster*," *PMLA*, XLI (1926), 294–303. J. E. Savage considers Sidney's *Arcadia* to be the main source, transmitted through an earlier Beaumont and Fletcher play, *Cupid's Revenge*; see his "Beaumont and Fletcher's *Philaster* and Sidney's *Arcadia*," *ELH*, XIV (1947), 194–206. A related article is Savage's "The Date of Beaumont and Fletcher's *Cupid's Revenge*," *ELH*, XV (1948), 286–294.

[13] J. F. Danby comments: "The main poetic feature of Beaumont and Fletcher is their adaptation to the stage of the sonneteer's material and the sonneteer's 'conceit'" (*Poets on Fortune's Hill* [London, 1952], p. 180).

[14] Harrison, "A Probable Source," p. 294. Fletcher's probable reading knowledge of Spanish is supported by Edward M. Wilson in two articles: "Did John Fletcher Read Spanish?" *Philological Quarterly*, XXVII (1948), 187–190; and *"Rule a Wife and Have a Wife* and *El Sagaz Estacio,"* *Review of English Studies*, XXIV (July, 1948), 189–194. Edna Earle Hobbs also attests to Fletcher's knowledge of Spanish in her Florida State University doctoral dissertation, "Spanish Influence on the Plays of Beaumont and Fletcher" (University Microfilms, 1963).

[15] Waith, *Pattern of Tragicomedy*, p. 3; there seems to be no evidence to support Mincoff's impression that *Philaster* predates *The*

INTRODUCTION

states that this play was "the earliest, and long remained the only, deliberate attempt to acclimatize upon the popular stage in England a pastoral drama which should occupy a position corresponding to that of Tasso and Guarini in Italy." Greg points out that, while Fletcher imitates the type of romance found in Tasso's *Aminta* (1572-73) and Guarini's *Il Pastor Fido* (or *The Faithful Shepherd*, published in 1589-90), his plot in *The Faithful Shepherdess* is largely independent both in general construction and in single incidents and characters.[16] He seems to have intended, in the best Renaissance tradition, to give English literature a worthy rival to the phenomenally successful Italian pastoral plays and to have witnessed with some bitterness the total failure of *The Faithful Shepherdess* on stage in the winter of 1608-9. His preface to the undated first quarto (ca. 1609-10) mentions audience misunderstanding of the purposes of pastoral tragicomedy as a reason for the failure of his play when acted, and goes on to define terms in a statement which has great value in the light it throws on Fletcher's concept of tragicomedy. But *The Faithful Shepherdess* was so woefully weak in dramatic techniques that no amount of audience sympathy could atone

Faithful Shepherdess (see n. 1, above). Other influential plays of a romantic-pastoral type may have been Shakespeare's *Pericles* (see, for example, Lawrence B. Wallis, *Fletcher, Beaumont, and Company, Entertainers to the Jacobean Gentry* [New York, 1947], pp. 169-171), Beaumont and Fletcher's *Cupid's Revenge* (see n. 12, above), and Shakespeare's *Cymbeline*. Ashley H. Thorndike in his pioneer study, *The Influence of Beaumont and Fletcher on Shakespeare* (Worcester, Mass., 1901), pp. 152-160, sees *Cymbeline* as being indebted to *Philaster*. Many recent critics agree with G. E. Bentley concerning the two plays that "it is their common purpose and environment, not imitation of one by the other, which makes them similar" ("Shakespeare and the Blackfriars Theatre," *Shakespeare Survey*, I [1948], p. 48). The much-discussed question of Beaumont and Fletcher's influence on Shakespeare "has, in fact, been warehoused rather than disposed of for good," according to E. M. W. Tillyard (*Shakespeare's Last Plays* [New York, 1964], p. 6). The probability is that Shakespeare, Beaumont, and Fletcher, creating plays for the same company of actors at the same time, knew each others' work before stage performance and publication, and swapped ideas in ways that can never be traced through modern-day comparisons of the printed texts.

[16] Greg, *Pastoral Poetry and Pastoral Drama* (London, 1906), pp. 265-266.

xviii

INTRODUCTION

for its faults. Waith calls it "stiffly artificial" and feels that the emotions of the play are "related only incidentally to character and plot"; Greg mentions "the priggish extravagance" of many passages in Fletcher's play.[17] Yet *The Faithful Shepherdess* contains many of the ingredients used later in the highly successful *Philaster*. William W. Appleton cites, for example, "the schematic conception" of the two plots, each made up of "two neatly designed triangles, one composed of virtuous characters . . . and the other made up of the activating villains of the piece."[18] Perigot, the hero of *The Faithful Shepherdess*, and Philaster vacillate between elation and despair;[19] and both wound their lovers when crass reality seems to be impinging on the ideal love for which the heroes yearn. Lawrence B. Wallis feels that the main lesson learned by Fletcher from the failure of his early play was to dispense with an emphatic controlling theme and to move toward "emotional patterning" as the integrating force in plot structure.[20]

Madeleine Doran calls Fletcher's statement on tragicomedy in his preface to *The Faithful Shepherdess* "the only important attempt at definition in England,"[21] even though it is a partial definition, intended principally to explain Fletcher's techniques in *The Faithful Shepherdess* and serving to prefigure his and Beaumont's further development of the type in *Philaster*. Here is Fletcher's statement:

> A tragi-comedy is not so called in respect of mirth and killing, but in respect it wants deaths, which is enough to make it no tragedy, yet brings some near it, which is enough to make it no comedy, which must be a representation of familiar people, with such kind of trouble as no life be questioned; so that a god is as lawful in this as in a tragedy, and mean people as in a comedy. Thus much

[17] Waith, *Pattern of Tragicomedy*, pp. 5, 10; Greg, *Pastoral Poetry*, p. 190, note.
[18] Appleton, *Beaumont and Fletcher, A Critical Study* (London, 1956), p. 29.
[19] Ibid., p. 30; see also p. 19.
[20] Wallis, *Fletcher, Beaumont, and Company*, pp. 189–190.
[21] Doran, *Endeavors of Art: A Study of Form in Elizabethan Drama* (Madison, Wisc., 1954), p. 208.

INTRODUCTION

I hope will serve to justify my poem, and make you understand it; to teach you more for nothing, I do not know that I am in conscience bound.[22]

Guarini's description of tragicomedy, almost certainly known to Fletcher, is "usefully applicable to Fletcher's plays," as Clifford Leech says, and lacks the testiness of a disappointed author which permeates Fletcher's statement. Guarini writes:

> He who composes tragicomedy takes from tragedy its great persons but not its great action, its verisimilar plot but not its true one, its movement of the feelings but not its disturbance of them, its pleasure but not its sadness, its danger but not its death; from comedy he takes laughter that is not excessive, modest amusement, feigned difficulty, happy reversal, and above all the comic order.[23]

Guarini claimed that his *tragi-commedia* was a new dramatic form,[24] and Beaumont and Fletcher were consciously offering a dramatic innovation in *Philaster*. It is true, as Waith points out, that Fletcherian tragicomedy is "something of an anomaly—almost another genre" and presents the difficulty of understanding "something which is unique."[25] Nevertheless, the eight hallmarks of tragicomedy listed by Waith in his detailed study of the genre are all found in *Philaster*: the imitation of the manners of the familiar world combined with a "theatrical" remoteness from that world, intricacy of plot, improbable hypotheses, an atmosphere of evil, Protean characters, and emotional intensity expressed in an artificial language of emotion.[26]

Leech's evaluation of this sort of drama is a fair one: "The world of tragicomedy is not a world of greatness destroyed but a world of little people in great positions, suffering distress but not ultimate disaster. It gives us a partial view of life, being

---

[22] The Variorum Edition of *The Works of Beaumont and Fletcher*, III (London, 1908), 18; the editor of *The Faithful Shepherdess* is W. W. Greg.

[23] Quoted in Clifford Leech, *The John Fletcher Plays* (Cambridge, Mass., 1962), p. 77.

[24] Greg, *Pastoral Poetry*, p. 201.

[25] Waith, *Pattern of Tragicomedy*, p. 43.

[26] Ibid., pp. 36–41.

INTRODUCTION

dependent, like comedy, on the exclusion of certain basic things in our existence."[27] Cyrus Hoy is surely correct in stating, in his far-ranging study of the effects of comedy, tragedy, and tragicomedy, *The Hyacinth Room*, that "the tragicomic dilemma of man is most effectively portrayed in the Jacobean drama in plays that are not, strictly speaking, tragicomedies."[28] Fletcherian tragicomedy, whether with pastoral characteristics as in *The Faithful Shepherdess* and *Philaster* or without them as in *A King and No King*, is a very special type of drama, unique in its fusing of elements drawn from varied sources. Waith believes that it makes its appeal, somewhat as abstract painting does, "directly to an emotional and aesthetic response." He concludes, rather pessimistically, that the net effect of Beaumont and Fletcher's blending of pastoral romance with tragicomedy "can be described as a major increase in formalization and a corresponding decrease in meaning."[29]

Even such a brief summary of the varied aspects of Beaumont and Fletcher tragicomedy as the foregoing may serve to illustrate the difficulty of understanding and judging the form. It is unlike any other tragicomedy, it is uniquely a Beaumont and Fletcher product, and it strikes all critics as being complex, diverse, and artificial—or at least basically lacking in truth to actual life. Waith adds yet another tradition which significantly influenced the two playwrights and which removes their tragicomedy further from real life. This is the rhetorical tradition transmitted by Seneca the Elder, father of the tragedian, who attended a school of declamation in Augustan Rome and, in *Oratorum et rhetorum sententiae, divisiones, colores*, recorded at the age of ninety what he could remember of the speeches he had heard. The work, still studied in English schools during Beaumont and Fletcher's time, is divided into ten books of *Controversiae*, or judicial declamations, and one book of *Suasoriae*, or deliberative declamations. As Waith describes the pedagogical method of the Roman schools, "the master (the *rhetor*) outlined a situation, either historical or more often purely fictitious, and told the students

[27] Leech, *John Fletcher Plays*, p. 82.
[28] Hoy, *The Hyacinth Room: An Investigation into the Nature of Comedy, Tragedy, and Tragicomedy* (New York, 1964), p. 213.
[29] Waith, *Pattern of Tragicomedy*, pp. 42, 85.

INTRODUCTION

what opinion each of them was to defend. They began with suasoriae, in which they imagined themselves deliberating with Alexander whether to launch his ships on the sea, or with Agamemnon whether to sacrifice Iphigenia. They then came to the more difficult controversiae, in which they imagined themselves in the forum, taking one side or the other in a legal battle."[30] The hypothetical situations became extravagant and led to ingenious masterpieces of declamation which were highly emotional ends in themselves. "In Fletcherian drama as in the Roman declamation," says Waith, "the challenge of a preposterous hypothesis is met with brilliant improvisation. No effort is spared to imagine what might happen in these extraordinary circumstances, or what strange motives might impel the protagonists toward further complications of a similar nature. At the crises one character confronts another to accuse him of disloyalty, ingratitude, or some other form of moral turpitude, in impassioned speech, glittering with all the resources of rhetoric." The quarrels in both Seneca and Beaumont and Fletcher are without real substance, and as soon as the situation is thoroughly exploited for dramatic effect, the hypothesis is demolished and the conflict ends.[31] Philaster's agonizing over the alleged falseness of Arethusa in III.i, and Dion's and Bellario's exchanges with him, are examples of emotional speeches based on purely hypothetical situations; so are the exchanges between Philaster and Arethusa in III.ii, especially Philaster's misogynist outburst at ll. 120–143. The wounding scenes in Act IV present perfect examples of extravagant speeches and actions without basis in logic or fact; once exploited for dramatic effect, as Waith has pointed out, such false hypotheses as Arethusa's unfaithfulness with Bellario are demolished and there is no conflict. The audience viewing a Beaumont and Fletcher play must have admired the ingenious verbal techniques, probably recognizing their Senecan nature, while at the same time being moved by the emotional intensity of the speeches. Thus another tradition employed by the two playwrights has the effect of moving their

---

[30] Ibid., p. 87.
[31] Waith, "John Fletcher and the Art of Declamation," *PMLA*, LXVI (1951), 232, 234.

INTRODUCTION

tragicomedies away from actuality and meaning and toward further formalization.[32]

There is, however, a certain cutting edge of satire in *Philaster* which compensates the modern reader a bit for the unreality of pastoral, tragicomic, and declamatory tradition. The old satyr plays, and satyr characters in later pastoral romances, had a connection with satire not only through accidental confusion of the terms but also because the rough satyrs usually took a mocking attitude somewhat as does Jaques in *As You Like It*.[33] Dramatic satire as practiced by Marston, Jonson, and Shakespeare can be similar to the mingling of satire and romance found in Beaumont and Fletcher's early plays, but the tone of Beaumont and Fletcher is unique. Waith, discussing Shakespeare's combination of satire and pastoral romance in *As You Like It*, remarks: "If Shakespeare does not fully accept the romantic conventions, neither does he altogether reject them. Rather than passing judgment on the pastoral ideal, he makes drama out of the witty interplay between two sets of conventions." On the other hand, Waith feels that "the effect of Beaumont and Fletcher's new tragicomedy depends . . . upon the obliteration of all clear lines of distinction, the imperceptible merging of one convention with another. Satyr and shepherd lose their identities here as completely as do tragedy and comedy."[34] Certainly it is hard to see in Dion's sophisticated mockery of the king's pretense of power the sort of satyr-like jibing exhibited by Jaques. Nor is the melancholic-jealous Philaster's wounding of Arethusa and Bellario much like the gentle pastoralism of Orlando as he posts his love poems to Rosalind on the trees in Arden. Yet for all the difference in tone these are probably variations on the same satiric-pastoral theme.

Clifford Leech is sensing a more subtle type of satire when he comments: "*Philaster*'s neat planning does not prevent the emergence of some degree of complexity in its feeling. The play does not disturb us, but it does comment on human pretences. The playwrights offer us a courtly romance, and offer us too their mockery if we will take its chief figures at

[32] Waith, *Pattern of Tragicomedy*, pp. 191, 98.
[33] Ibid., pp. 43–85 (Chapter II, "Satyr and Shepherd").
[34] Ibid., p. 83.

xxiii

INTRODUCTION

their own valuation. Its laughter is not excessive, as Guarini decreed for tragicomedy, but such laughter as there is contributes powerfully to the total effect."[35] This would indeed be a new wrinkle in dramatic satire, if to the overt mockery of the king by Dion is to be added the authors' mockery of Swinburne-like critics who respond too subjectively to the "loveliest if not the loftiest" aspects of pastoral nobility in *Philaster*. But it is quite possibly a facet of the unique tone of Beaumont and Fletcher. Beaumont had shown himself to be an extremely able satirist in *The Knight of the Burning Pestle*; and the Jacobean gentlemen who patronized the Blackfriars Theatre when *Philaster* was being performed would have had a sympathetic understanding of the young prince's petulant nobleness which they might well have lacked when the foibles of the citizen and his wife were on display in the earlier play.

The satirical play which most clearly foreshadows *Philaster* is John Marston's *The Malcontent* (1604). Wallis points out many general similarities such as the court settings, aristocratic characters, comic elements, and stressing of sexual passions. Also noted by Wallis are similar characterizations: the lustful, vicious Megra and Pietro's duchess; swaggering Pharamond and Machiavellian Mendoza; the wronged prince Philaster and the true duke Giovanni, in disguise as Malevole; the faithful friends and the usurpers in both plays. *The Malcontent* features the theatrical non-fatal stabbing of a gallant and a hunting expedition with forest scenes. Totally lacking in Marston's play, of course, are true pastoral elements and especially the theme of young love.[36] Beaumont and Fletcher seem here to be reflecting the influence of the "comical satire" developed by Marston and Ben Jonson to substitute for the prose and poetic satires banished by an edict of the bishops in 1599.[37] As O. J. Campbell points out, "The experiments of these two dramatists had established a number of new conventions. They had devised an improved stage for the exhibition and deflation of most of the gulls and knaves who had appeared in the banished

[35] Leech, *John Fletcher Plays*, p. 94.
[36] Wallis, *Fletcher, Beaumont, and Company*, p. 168.
[37] Oscar James Campbell, *Comicall Satyre and Shakespeare's "Troilus and Cressida"* (San Marino, 1938), p. vii.

satires. They had welcomed, in particular, the old crowd of social pretenders and gulls and had retained the same severity toward sins of sex. . . . They had presented the exposure of the gulls as resulting either in public renunciation of their aberrations . . . or in their scornful dismissal following their humiliation—as it were, their ejection from the play."[38] In particular, Dion's harassing of Pharamond and Megra, his determination to expose their lustful relationship, and the humiliation of the two culprits at the end of the play seem to be clearly in the tradition of "comical satire."

There is, in addition, a complicated pattern of satire underlying the political scenes in *Philaster* which almost defies statement. The citizens who are ready to rebel against a usurping king for Philaster are both scorned and used by the courtly group;[39] Dion jibes at royal pretense as seen in the false king yet presumably wants Philaster as a "true" king in his place; Philaster is respectful toward the insurrectionists yet scornful of the honest Country Fellow; the affair between Pharamond and Megra and Philaster's dastardly treatment of Arethusa and Bellario display a moral weakness at court. It has been suggested that the key to this seemingly patternless commentary on court and town may lie in Beaumont and Fletcher's reactions to the conflicts of their own world. They basically lack the motivation which Campbell attributes to Marston and Jonson, to "arouse thoughtful laughter which would sharpen the social sense of their audience and clarify its moral judgments."[40] One influential critic, John F. Danby, believes that Beaumont and Fletcher's "best work is done where their main interest lies—

[38] Ibid., p. 183.

[39] Mary G. M. Adkins ("The Citizens in *Philaster*: Their Function and Significance," *Studies in Philology*, XLIII [1946], 203–212) believes that the citizens are in fact the dominant force in the political aspect of the plot, since their uprising provides the means by which the usurping king is deposed, Philaster restored, and Pharamond sent back to Spain. She notes that courtiers like Dion who are quietly responsible for the rebellion have the usual aristocratic contempt for the temperaments and intelligence of the common people, but Philaster treats them with respect and courtesy. Thus the play may show "the direction of the political winds in early seventeenth-century England."

[40] Campbell, *Comicall Satyre*, p. 184.

Introduction

in the conflict of the absolutes and the contortions it imposes on human nature."[41]

Danby's pursuit of his theory leads him to a somewhat unfortunate denigration both of Beaumont and Fletcher and the Jacobean world: "The *déclassé* son of the Bishop and the younger son of the Judge are James's unconscious agents. They are capturing the Great House literature [of Elizabethan tradition] for the courtier, writing for adherents of a Stuart king rather than for Tudor aristocrats. Their work, from one point of view, represents a snobbish vulgarization and a sectional narrowing of the great tradition." Yet Danby feels that their plays, for better or for worse, "strike roots deep into a real world—the world of their time and of the embryonic Cavalier."[42] Philaster prefigures the Cavalier as he sees himself a fated hero adrift in a world where the old values have lost their meaning. Kings are no longer omnipotent and benevolent, citizens are not necessarily faithful to the death, true love can seem to be crassly false, the glittering court can be rotten with corruption. As Appleton puts it, "Philaster has strayed into the no-man's-land of the dispossessed"; he is "the lost prince in search of an absolute." In this view, the wanderings of Arethusa, Bellario, and Philaster in Act IV become symbolic of "isolated individuals in a disassociated society."[43] The playwrights, especially Beaumont, seem to Danby to be adolescent and to have created an "all-or-nothing" world of adolescent intensities.[44]

It must be remembered, however, that this is the world of John Donne, whose agonized expression in poems like *An Anatomy of the World: The First Anniversary* (published in 1611, perhaps a year after *Philaster*'s composition) of the same dispossession seems anything but adolescent:

> 'Tis all in pieces, all coherence gone;
> All just supply, and all relation:
> Prince, subject, father, son, are things forgot.

---

[41] Danby, *Poets on Fortune's Hill*, p. 166.
[42] Ibid., pp. 157, 161.
[43] Appleton, *Beaumont and Fletcher*, pp. 30, 32.
[44] Danby, *Poets on Fortune's Hill*, p. 165.

INTRODUCTION

The problems of a world in the throes of conflict and change are common to Donne, the poet and preacher, and Beaumont and Fletcher, the brilliant young writers of tragicomedy. It is inevitable that the playwrights, creating for their Jacobean audience a new dramatic form uniquely different from Elizabethan tragedy and comedy, would have seen in their suffering hero's situation parallels with tension-ridden lives around them. That they chose not to stress the theme of isolation or dispossession or "conflicting absolutes" does not make them necessarily adolescent or opportunistic; they are simply not Donnes, as they are not Shakespeares, Marlowes, or even "sons of Ben." The Beaumont and Fletcher world is almost as remote as the Forest of Arden; only in a casual way does it relate to the Jacobean world in which the playwrights actually lived. They are playwrights who may very well, as Clifford Leech suspects, "offer us . . . their mockery if we will take [*Philaster*'s] chief figures at their own valuation." In their major plays, Leech believes, "we are never allowed to think only in one way about anything"; this drama "always withdraws from a final judgment: it is too sceptical ever to be rebellious: it refrains from assertion as from challenge."[45] Their critics should perhaps also refrain.

The tracing of influences on *Philaster* and of critical theories about the play's diverse elements attempted here may seem barren in that it does not readily lead to an acceptable valuation of Beaumont and Fletcher's work. It provides at least a fascinating view of two talented playwrights, hitherto unsuccessful, who pooled every resource at their command to create in *Philaster* a play continuously popular throughout the seventeenth century. It will never again be a truly popular play, despite Danby's impression that "Beaumont and Fletcher are, in an unfortunate sense, the first of the moderns," somewhat analogous with Byron in the nineteenth century and Graham Greene in the twentieth.[46] Critics who profess to see in Beaumont and Fletcher's plays some promise of popularity in the modern world too often base their opinions on a negative

[45] Leech, *John Fletcher Plays*, p. 47.
[46] Danby, *Poets on Fortune's Hill*, p. 183.

INTRODUCTION

view of both Jacobean and modern taste. Appleton, for instance, remarks: "Their fondness for sensation and shock, their emphasis on sex, their energy, brilliance and wit, even their coarseness, all recommend them to the modern temper."[47] In quite another vein, the late poet laureate John Masefield wrote admiringly of Beaumont and Fletcher as "among our ten best poets, whether for skill, invention, or range," lamented the rareness either of reading or performing the plays, and mentioned with wistful hope that "sooner or later, old beauties are rediscovered . . . ."[48] Many critics feel, however, that an unusual approach to *Philaster* would be necessary for appreciative viewing by a modern audience. Waith, for example, comments: "One may speculate that if a modern audience approached Beaumont and Fletcher with the expectations it has on going to the opera, it would find much to enjoy, for it would accept the contrivance of the play more readily and would await the more declamatory passages as eagerly as the famous arias, duets, or quartets of grand opera." It is Waith's contention that "sheer technical virtuosity" makes Beaumont and Fletcher's hypothetical situations and sharply delineated conflicts superb though extreme examples of dramatic formalism.[49] And Clifford Leech states his conviction that what is conveyed by a Beaumont and Fletcher play "is no sense of an important revelation of the nature of things: what appears is rather an intricate presentation of the patterns in which things can arrange themselves. The more intricate the presentation, the more it satisfied—we can feel sure enough—Fletcher's sense of how things were."[50]

It is doubtful that a modern audience could ever be brought to understand or agree with Beaumont and Fletcher's highly individual senses of "how things were," but *Philaster* could be performed as entertainingly as *As You Like It* and *Twelfth Night* sometimes are. Its principal lure, however, will continue to lie in its fascination for critics, who reflect the playwrights' intricacies in their own diverse theories about the play. Off in the

---

[47] Appleton, *Beaumont and Fletcher*, p. 118.
[48] John Masefield, "Beaumont and Fletcher," *The Atlantic*, CXCIX (June, 1957), 71–74.
[49] Waith, *Pattern in Tragicomedy*, p. 201.
[50] Leech, *John Fletcher Plays*, p. 141.

wings can still be heard Beaumont and Fletcher's mocking laughter not only at those of us who "take *Philaster*'s chief figures at their own valuation" but at those who believe that one critical theory can ever cover the myriad facets of this enigmatic play.

THE TEXT

Appropriately, the text of *Philaster* offers enough unsolved problems to reflect the customary difficulty in arriving at a satisfactory view of the play. The puzzling questions concerning the texts of the two earliest quartos have never been settled and perhaps never can be. Robert K. Turner, editor of *Philaster* for the Beaumont and Fletcher works currently being issued by the Cambridge University Press, has subjected the early texts to their most careful bibliographical scrutiny and has probably established all the facts that can be established on the basis of present knowledge. Here is Turner's summary of information about early editions of *Philaster*.[51]

Edition	Date	Publisher(s)	Printer	Set from
Q1	1620	Walkley	Okes	MS
Q2	1622	Walkley	Okes	Q1 [plus MSS]
Q3	1628	Hawkins	Mathewes	Q2
Q4	1634	Hawkins	Jones	Q3
Q5	1639	Leake	Griffin	Q4
Q6	1652	Leake	?	Q5
Q7	ca. 1661	Kirkman	Johnson	Q6
Q8	after 1661	Leake	?	Q6
F2	1679	Mariot et al.	Macock	Q8
Q9	1687	Bentley and Magnes	?	Q3

Only Q1 and Q2 seem to have any manuscript authority. Of the editions after Q2, Turner notes: "A comparison . . . reveals little more than the progressive degeneration of the text that is inevitable in a long series of reprints."[52]

[51] Turner, ed., *Philaster* (Cambridge, 1966), p. 370.
[52] Ibid., p. 371.

Introduction

Thomas Walkley, the publisher of both Q1 and Q2, admitted the deficiencies of the first edition's text but not their cause in his preface to Q2:

> Courteous Reader. *Philaster* and *Arethusa* his love have lain so long ableeding, by reason of some dangerous and gaping wounds which they received in the first impression, that it is wondered how they could go abroad so long or travel so far as they have done. Although they were hurt neither by me nor the printer, yet I, knowing and finding by experience how many well-wishers they have abroad, have adventured to bind up their wounds and to enable them to visit upon better terms such friends of theirs as were pleased to take knowledge of them, so maimed and deformed as they at the first were; and if they were then gracious in your sight, assuredly they will now find double favor, being reformed and set forth suitable to their birth and breeding.

Partly on the basis of Walkley's reference to the "dangerous and gaping wounds" of Q1, Leo Kirschbaum identified this text as a bad quarto; that is, a memorially reconstructed text.[53] Subsequent efforts to prove or disprove Kirschbaum's contention have been inconclusive, although Turner states: "I am inclined, but with some reservations, to think it a bad text."[54] The first eighty-six lines of the Q1 text and the last six quarto-pages present a version of the play almost entirely different from Q2, leading Alexander Dyce, an early editor of *Philaster*, to suggest that these "portions must have been supplied 'for the nonce' by some hireling writer."[55] The probability is that the Q1 manu-

---

[53] Kirschbaum, "A Census of Bad Quartos," *Review of English Studies*, XIV (1938), 20–43.

[54] Turner, *Philaster*, p. 396. Agreeing with Kirschbaum that Q1 is reported is J. W. Hughes in "A Textual Study of Beaumont and Fletcher's *Philaster*" (Ph.D. dissertation, University of Iowa, 1948). My own doctoral dissertation, "A Survey of Non-Shakespearean Bad Quartos" (University of Virginia, 1953), includes a brief note on *Philaster* (Appendix A, pp. 230–243) which suggests that evidence for reporting is not conclusive. Both of these dissertations have been published by University Microfilms.

[55] Dyce, *The Works of Beaumont and Fletcher*, I (London, 1843), 198.

Introduction

script had been damaged at beginning and end and could be rendered usable only through non-authorial supply writing; and the central portions of the Q1 text, which closely parallel Q2 but vary in lineation and in many readings, exhibit enough errors to warrant Turner's statement that the entire quarto "must have been set up from a truly miserable manuscript."[56] Q2, the copy-text for all editions of *Philaster*, including the present one, was set from a heavily annotated copy of Q1 except for the initial and concluding lines, which were set directly from the manuscript. Turner believes this manuscript to have been "either the prompt-book or authorial fair copy or a transcript of one of them."[57] Q1 readings are followed by modern editors only when Q2 appears to be clearly in error.

J. E. Savage believes that Q1 represents an authorized London stage version which has been considerably revised for reasons of censorship.[58] Savage points out that Q2 references to the king's "joint kingdoms" of Sicily and Calabria have disappeared from the rewritten first scene of Q1 and that similar topics likely to irritate King James have been cut both in the rewritten parts and the parallel central portions of the text. Peter Davison notes that Q1 omits much of the brutal baiting of the Spanish prince Pharamond, perhaps reflecting James's desire for peace with Spain.[59] Some censorship, or expedient softening, for political reasons seems possible, but the primary motive for rewriting portions of Q1 must have been to repair a damaged manuscript.

The present edition is based on microfilm of the Huntington Library copy of Q2. One of the two copies of Q1 in the Huntington Library has also been consulted on microfilm (C1681/60257). A departure from the usual editorial practice in plays in the Regents Renaissance Drama Series is that textual variants are not given above the line on each page of text. Instead, Appendix A presents a modern-spelling version of the beginning and ending of the Q1 text, and Appendix B lists the principal substantive variants between the present text, usually the Q2

---

[56] Turner, *Philaster*, p. 375.
[57] Ibid., p. 380.
[58] See note 1 above for information about Savage's article.
[59] Davison, "Serious Concerns," p. 13; cited in n. 1 above.

INTRODUCTION

version, and other early texts. Of these, Q3 has been consulted on microfilm from the Beinecke Rare Book and Manuscript Library of Yale University, and Q4–9 and Folio 2 on microfilm from the Folger Shakespeare Library. Press variants in extant copies of Q1 and Q2, and emendation of accidentals in early texts, have not been listed; they may be found, together with a detailed historical collation of substantive variants, in Turner's edition.

My thanks are due the libraries whose staffs have kindly supplied me with materials for this study; to those mentioned above should be added the Alderman Library at the University of Virginia and the Lynchburg College Library. Lynchburg College provided me with two research grants to support my work; one of these was in part supported by the Ford Foundation for the Advancement of Education.

DORA JEAN ASHE

Lynchburg College

PHILASTER

PERSONS REPRESENTED IN THE PLAY

THE KING
PHILASTER, *heir to the crown*
PHARAMOND, *Prince of Spain*
DION, *a lord*
CLEREMONT
THRASILINE } *noble gentlemen his associates*
ARETHUSA, *the King's daughter*
GALATEA, *a wise modest lady attending the princess*
MEGRA, *a lascivious lady*
ANOTHER LADY *attending the princess*
EUPHRASIA, daughter of Dion, but disguised like a page, and called
  BELLARIO
AN OLD CAPTAIN
FIVE CITIZENS
A COUNTRY FELLOW
TWO WOODMEN
THE KING'S GUARD AND TRAIN

The Scene being in Sicily

There is no list of characters in Q2; the list in Q1 is briefer than that given here. The present version is adapted from the Second Folio; a similar listing is found in Q3–9. Dropped here, but appearing in most of the listings, is a "ghost" character described as "An old wanton lady, or crone." Spelling of characters' names is approximately that of Q3–9 and F. Q1 spellings are given in Appendix A. Q2 usually employs the spelling *Arathusa* for *Arethusa*, *Trasiline* for *Thrasiline* (Q3 *Thrasaline*), *Gallatea* for *Galatea*, sometimes *Clerimond* for *Cleremont*. Turner discusses compositorial and authorial preferences in spelling characters' names in his Textual Notes, pp. 485–486.

Philaster

or

Love Lies a-Bleeding

[I.i] *Enter* Dion, Cleremont, *and* Thrasiline.

CLEREMONT.
Here's nor lords nor ladies.
DION.
Credit me, gentlemen, I wonder at it. They receiv'd strict charge from the king to attend here. Besides, it was boldly published that no officer should forbid any gentlemen that desired to attend and hear. 5
CLEREMONT.
Can you guess the cause?
DION.
Sir, it is plain, about the Spanish prince that's come to marry our kingdom's heir and be our sovereign.
THRASILINE.
Many that will seem to know much, say she looks not on him like a maid in love. 10
DION.
Faith, sir, the multitude, that seldom know anything but their own opinions, speak that they would have. But the prince, before his own approach, receiv'd so many confident messages from the state that I think she's resolv'd to be rul'd. 15
CLEREMONT.
Sir, it is thought with her he shall enjoy both these kingdoms of Sicily and Calabria.

---

1. *nor . . . nor*] neither . . . nor.
2. *that*] what.

17 *Calabria*] the "heel of the boot"; in modern times (since the eighth century) a territorial district in the southern extremity of Italy,

I.i] PHILASTER

DION.
 Sir, it is without controversy so meant. But 'twill be a troublesome labor for him to enjoy both these kingdoms with safety, the right heir to one of them living, and living so virtuously; especially the people admiring the bravery of his mind and lamenting his injuries. 20

CLEREMONT.
 Who, Philaster?

DION.
 Yes, whose father we all know was by our late king of Calabria unrighteously deposed from his fruitful Sicily. 25 Myself drew some blood in those wars which I would give my hand to be washed from.

CLEREMONT.
 Sir, my ignorance in state policy will not let me know why, Philaster being heir to one of these kingdoms, the king should suffer him to walk abroad with such free 30 liberty.

DION.
 Sir, it seems your nature is more constant than to inquire after state news. But the king of late made a hazard of both the kingdoms, of Sicily and his own, with offering but to imprison Philaster. At which the city was in 35 arms, not to be charm'd down by any state order or proclamation till they saw Philaster ride through the streets pleas'd and without a guard; at which they threw their hats and their arms from them, some to make bonfires, some to drink, all for his deliverance. Which wise 40 men say is the cause the king labors to bring in the power of a foreign nation, to awe his own with.

   Enter Galatea, *a* Lady, *and* Megra.

---

bounded on the north by the province of Potenza (Lucania) and on the other sides by the sea; generally now called the Sila in contradistinction to the Aspromonte *(Encyclopedia Britannica).*

 33. *made a hazard of*] risked losing.

 38. *pleas'd*] "Can the true reading be 'released'?" (Dyce).

 42.1.] Q2–9 and F read, "*Enter* Galatea, Megra, *and a* Lady." Theobald, as suggested by Seward and followed by most later editors, emends to the reading given here to agree with Dion's description

—6—

THRASILINE.
See, the ladies! What's the first?
DION.
A wise and modest gentlewoman that attends the princess. 45
CLEREMONT.
The second?
DION.
She is one that may stand still discreetly enough and ill favor'dly dance her measure, simper when she is courted by her friend, and slight her husband.
CLEREMONT.
The last? 50
DION.
Faith, I think she is one whom the state keeps for the agents of our confederate princess. She'll cog and lie with a whole army, before the league shall break. Her name is common through the kingdom, and the trophies of her dishonor advanc'd beyond Hercules' Pillars. She 55 loves to try the several constitutions of men's bodies, and indeed she has destroyed the worth of her own body by making experiment upon it for the good of the commonwealth.
CLEREMONT.
She's a profitable member. 60
MEGRA.
Peace, if you love me. You shall see these gentlemen stand their ground and not court us.

---

of the *first, second* and *last* ladies, since the *last* seems to be Megra. The present edition also follows Theobald in assigning the Lady's speeches to Megra and vice versa. Turner follows Theobald in emending the order of names in the stage direction but retains the speech prefixes of Q2.

48. *measure*] "a dance, especially a grave or stately dance" (OED).
52. *cog*] "to employ fraud or deceit to cheat, originally at dice" *(OED)*.
55. *Hercules' Pillars*] "the rocks Calpé (now Gibraltar) and Abyla (Ceuta), on either side of the Strait of Gibraltar, thought by the ancients to be the supports of the western boundary of the world, and to have been set up by Hercules" *(OED)*.

I.i PHILASTER

GALATEA.
  What if they should?
LADY.
  What if they should?
MEGRA.
  Nay, let her alone. What if they should? Why, if they should, I say they were never abroad. What foreigner would do so? It writes them directly untravel'd.
GALATEA.
  Why, what if they be?
LADY.
  What if they be?
MEGRA.
  Good madam, let her go on. What if they be? Why, if they be, I will justify they cannot maintain discourse with a judicious lady, nor make a leg, nor say "excuse me."
GALATEA.
  Ha, ha, ha!
MEGRA.
  Do you laugh, madam?
DION.
  Your desires upon you, ladies.
MEGRA.
  Then you must sit beside us.
DION.
  I shall sit near you then, lady.
MEGRA.
  Near me perhaps. But there's a lady endures no stranger, and to me you appear a very strange fellow.
LADY.
  Methinks he's not so strange. He would quickly to be acquainted.
THRASILINE.
  Peace, the king!

  Enter King, Pharamond, *Arethusa, and train.*

---
  72. *make a leg*] bow.

KING.
    To give a stronger testimony of love
    Than sickly promises, which commonly　　　　　85
    In princes find both birth and burial
    In one breath, we have drawn you, worthy sir,
    To make your fair endearments to our daughter
    And worthy services known to our subjects,
    Now lov'd and wonder'd at. Next, our intent　　　90
    To plant you deeply our immediate heir
    Both to our blood and kingdoms. For this lady
    (The best part of your life, as you confirm me
    And I believe), though her few years and sex
    Yet teach her nothing but her fears and blushes,　95
    Desires without desire, discourse and knowledge
    Only of what herself is to herself,
    Make her feel moderate health; and when she sleeps,
    In making no ill day, knows no ill dreams.
    Think not, dear sir, these undivided parts　　　100
    That must mold up a virgin are put on
    To show her so, as borrowed ornaments,
    To talk of her perfect love to you, or add
    An artificial shadow to her nature.
    No, sir, I boldly dare proclaim her yet　　　　105
    No woman. But woo her still and think her modesty
    A sweeter mistress than the offer'd language
    Of any dame, were she a queen, whose eye
    Speaks common loves and comforts to her servants.
    Last, noble son (for so I now must call you),　110
    What I have done thus public is not only
    To add a comfort in particular

---

96. *discourse*] reason or judgment; "perhaps . . . a more rapid deduction of consequences from premises, than was supposed to be effected by reason . . ." (Dyce, quoting Gifford's edition of Massinger). Daniel suggests that the word "be considered as merely expletive" when coupled with terms like reason, judgment, and knowledge.

103. *talk of*] speak.

107. *A sweeter . . . language*] Correspondence between Q1 and Q2 texts begins with this line.

109. *servants*] lovers; "the title which ladies formerly bestowed on their professed and authorized admirers" (Dyce).

I.i PHILASTER

To you or me, but all; and to confirm
The nobles and the gentry of these kingdoms
By oath to your succession, which shall be   115
Within this month at most.

THRASILINE.
This will be hardly done.   [*They speak aside.*]
CLEREMONT.
It must be ill done, if it be done.
DION.
When 'tis at best, 'twill be but half done whilst so brave
a gentleman is wrong'd and flung off.   120
THRASILINE.
I fear.
CLEREMONT.
Who does not?
DION.
I fear not for myself and yet I fear, too. Well, we shall
see, we shall see. No more.
PHARAMOND.
Kissing your white hand, mistress, I take leave   125
To thank your royal father and thus far
To be my own free trumpet. Understand,
Great king, and these your subjects, mine that must be
(For so deserving you have spoke me, sir,
And so deserving I dare speak myself).   130
To what a person, of what eminence,
Ripe expectation, of what faculties,
Manners and virtues you would wed your kingdoms.
You in me have your wishes. Oh, this country!
By more than all the gods I hold it happy: 135
Happy in their dear memories that have been
Kings great and good; happy in yours that is;
And from you, as a chronicle to keep
Your noble name from eating age, do I
Open myself most happy. Gentlemen,   140

---

140. *Open myself*] so Q1–9; the F reading, *opine myself,* is followed by most editors except Turner. Theobald emends to "opine it in myself." *Open* seems appropriate to Pharamond's most happily offering himself as an entry in a chronicle history to preserve the succession and hence the present king's reputation.

—10—

Believe me in a word, a prince's word,
There shall be nothing to make up a kingdom
Mighty and flourishing, defensed, fear'd,
Equal to be commanded and obey'd,
But through the travails of my life I'll find it   145
And tie it to this country. By all the gods,
My reign shall be so easy to the subject
That every man shall be his prince himself
And his own law; yet I his prince and law.
And dearest lady, to your dearest self   150
(Dear in the choice of him whose name and luster
Must make you more and mightier) let me say,
You are the blessed'st living; for, sweet princess,
You shall enjoy a man of men to be
Your servant. You shall make him yours for whom   155
Great queens must die.

THRASILINE.
Miraculous!

CLEREMONT.
This speech calls him Spaniard, being nothing but a large inventory of his own commendations.

DION.
I wonder what's his price? For certainly he'll sell him-   160
self, he has so prais'd his shape.

Enter Philaster.

But here comes one more worthy those large speeches than the large speaker of them. Let me be swallow'd quick if I can find in all the anatomy of yon man's virtues one sinew sound enough to promise for him he   165
shall be constable. By this sun, he'll ne'er make king, unless it be of trifles, in my poor judgment.

PHILASTER.
Right noble sir, as low as my obedience
And with a heart as loyal as my knee,
I beg your favor.

KING.   Rise, you have it, sir.   170

---

164. *quick*] alive.

I.i   PHILASTER

DION.
    Mark but the king, how pale he looks. He fears.
    Oh, this same whoreson Conscience, how it jades us!
KING.
    Speak your intents, sir.
PHILASTER.   Shall I speak 'em freely?
    Be still my royal sovereign.
KING.   As a subject,
    We give you freedom.   175
DION [*aside*].
    Now it heats.
PHILASTER.
    Then thus I turn
    My language to you, prince, you foreign man.
    Ne'er stare nor put on wonder, for you must
    Endure me and you shall. This earth you tread upon,   180
    A dowry as you hope with this fair princess,
    By my dead father (oh, I had a father
    Whose memory I bow to) was not left
    To your inheritance, and I up and living
    Having myself about me and my sword,   185
    The souls of all my name and memories,
    These arms and some few friends, beside the gods,
    To part so calmly with it and sit still
    And say I might have been. I tell thee, Pharamond,
    When thou art king, look I be dead and rotten   190
    And my name ashes, as I. For hear me, Pharamond,
    This very ground thou goest on, this fat earth
    My father's friends made fertile with their faiths,
    Before that day of shame shall gape and swallow
    Thee and thy nation like a hungry grave   195

---

172. *jades*] tires, wears out *(OED)*.
182–183. *By . . . left*] In Q1–9 and F the order of these lines is reversed. They were transposed by Theobald, followed by Dyce and later editors. The original order seems clearly incorrect, since the clause *whose memory I bow to* then refers to Princess Arethusa rather than to Philaster's dead father.
192. *fat*] fertile, rich *(OED)*.
193. *made . . . faiths*] enriched with their blood.

—12—

Into her hidden bowels. Prince, it shall!
By the just gods it shall!
PHARAMOND. He's mad, beyond cure mad.
DION [*aside*].
Here's a fellow has some fire in's veins.
The outlandish prince looks like a tooth-drawer.
PHILASTER.
Sir prince of popinjays, I'll make it well appear   200
To you I am not mad.
KING. You displease us.
You are too bold.
PHILASTER. No, sir, I am too tame,
Too much a turtle, a thing born without passion,
A faint shadow that every drunken cloud sails over
And makes nothing.
KING. I do not fancy this.   205
Call our physicians! Sure he's somewhat tainted.
THRASILINE.
I do not think 'twill prove so.
DION.
He's given him a general purge already, for all the right
he has, and now he means to let him blood. Be constant,
gentlemen. By heaven, I'll run his hazard although I run   210
my name out of the kingdom.
CLEREMONT.
Peace, we are all one soul.
PHARAMOND.
What you have seen in me to stir offense
I cannot find, unless it be this lady
Offer'd into my arms with the succession   215

---

199. *a tooth-drawer*] proverbial expression for a thin, meager, or pale person (Daniel).

200. *popinjays*] "an early name for a parrot" *(OED)*.

206. *tainted*] "having a taint of disease; infected with latent disease" *(OED)*; here, mentally deranged.

209. *let him blood*] to bleed Philaster; the king's robbing of Philaster is compared in this passage with the treatment of disease through draining, as in purging and bleeding.

210. *run his hazard*] to run extreme risks (Onions), from a dice game called hazard.

I.i   PHILASTER

    Which I must keep; though it hath pleas'd your fury
    To mutiny within you, without disputing
    Your genealogies or taking knowledge
    Whose branch you are, the king will leave it me,
    And I dare make it mine. You have your answer.   220
PHILASTER.
    If thou wert sole inheritor to him
    That made the world his and couldst see no sun
    Shine upon anything but thine, were Pharamond
    As truly valiant as I feel him cold
    And ring'd amongst the choicest of his friends,   225
    Such as would blush to talk such serious follies
    Or back such belied commendations,
    And from this presence, spite of all these bugs,
    You shall hear further from me.
KING.   Sir, you wrong the prince.
    I gave you not this freedom to brave our best friends.   230
    You deserve our frown. Go to, be better temper'd.
PHILASTER.
    It must be, sir, when I am nobler us'd.
GALATEA [aside].
    Ladies, this would have been a pattern of succession
    Had he ne'er met this mischief. By my life,
    He is the worthiest the true name of man   235
    This day within my knowledge.
MEGRA.
    I cannot tell what you may call your knowledge,
    But th'other is the man set in my eye.

---

    222. *That . . . his*] Alexander the Great (Theobald).
    227. *belied*] so Q1–2, followed by Turner; Q3–9 and F, *bellied,* followed by most editors. *Belied* can signify "filled with lies," as in *Cymbeline,* III.iv.38: "'tis slander . . . whose breath/ Rides on the posting winds, and doth belie/ All corners of the world" *(OED).* Since *belied* is a possible reading and stands in the two early quartos, there seems to be no necessity for emending to *bellied* (inflated, puffed).
    228. *bugs*] hobgoblins, bogeys, imaginary objects of terror (Onions).
    233. *a pattern of succession*] ". . . Philaster might have been a pattern to succeeding Kings, had he not fall'n under the Misfortune of having his Right to the Kingdom usurp'd upon" (Theobald).

Oh, 'tis a prince of wax!
GALATEA. A dog it is.
KING. Philaster, tell me
The injuries you aim at in your riddles. 240
PHILASTER.
If you had my eyes, sir, and sufferance,
My griefs upon you, and my broken fortunes,
My wants great and now nothing, hopes and fears,
My wrongs would make ill riddles to be laugh'd at.
Dare you be still my king and right me? 245
KING.
Give me your wrongs in private.
PHILASTER. Take them
And ease me of a load would bow strong Atlas.
They whisper.
CLEREMONT.
He dares not stand the shock.
DION.
I cannot blame him; there's danger in't. Every man in
this age has not a soul of crystal for all men to read their 250
actions through. Men's hearts and faces are so far
asunder that they hold no intelligence. Do but view yon
stranger well and you shall see a fever through all his
bravery, and feel him shake like a true tenant. If he give
not back his crown again upon the report of an elder- 255
gun, I have no augury.

---

239. *a prince of wax*] perfectly molded, like a wax image. Cf. "a man of wax" in *Romeo and Juliet*, I.iii.76.

239. *A dog it is*] "The intention of Galatea's speech is obvious enough: instead of being a *prince of wax* Pharamond is but a *dog of wax*, an insignificant thing" (Daniel). Dyce cites the derogatory phrase "a dog of wax" in Ben Jonson's *Tale of a Tub*, II.ii; Daniel finds further occurrences in *Sir John Oldcastle*, II.ii.29, and *The Miseries of Enforced Marriage*, I.ii.

247. *Atlas*] Greek god, a Titan, who bore the world on his shoulders.

252. *intelligence*] communication or intercourse (Onions).

254. *like . . . tenant*] "like one who has only temporary possession" (Dyce). Theobald emends to *true recreant;* Daniel accepts the Q1 reading, *truant;* Turner follows Q2, *tenant*.

255–256. *elder-gun*] "a pop-gun made of a hollow shoot of elder [wood]" *(OED)*.

256. *augury*] power of prophecy.

KING.
>Go to. Be more yourself, as you respect our favor;
>You'll stir us else. Sir, I must have you know
>That y'are and shall be at our pleasure, what fashion we
>Will put upon you. Smooth your brow, or by the gods— 260

PHILASTER.
>I am dead, sir; y'are my fate. It was not I
>Said I was wrong'd. I carry all about me
>My weak stars lead me to, all my weak fortunes.
>Who dares in all this presence speak (that is
>But man of flesh and may be mortal), tell me 265
>I do not most entirely love this prince
>And honor his full virtues!

KING.   Sure, he's possess'd.

PHILASTER.
>Yes, with my father's spirit. It's here, oh king,
>A dangerous spirit. Now he tells me, king,
>I was a king's heir, bids me be a king, 270
>And whispers to me, these are all my subjects.
>'Tis strange, he will not let me sleep but dives
>Into my fancy and there gives me shapes
>That kneel and do me service, cry me king.
>But I'll suppress him; he's a factious spirit 275
>And will undo me. [*To* Pharamond.] Noble sir, your hand;
>I am your servant.

KING.   Away, I do not like this.
>I'll make you tamer or I'll dispossess you
>Both of life and spirit. For this time
>I pardon your wild speech, without so much 280
>As your imprisonment.

Exeunt King, Pharamond, *Arethusa.*

DION.
>I thank you, sir. You dare not for the people.

GALATEA.
>Ladies, what think you now of this brave fellow?

---

275. *factious*] contentious, given to faction.
282. *for*] because of.

MEGRA.
>   A pretty talking fellow, hot at hand. But eye yon
>   stranger; is he not a fine complete gentleman? Oh these 285
>   strangers, I do affect them strangely. They do the rarest
>   home things and please the fullest. As I live, I could love
>   all the nation over and over for his sake.

GALATEA.
>   Gods comfort your poor head-piece, lady. 'Tis a weak one
>   and had need of a night cap. *Exeunt* Ladies. 290

DION.
>   See how his fancy labors. Has he not spoke
>   Home, and bravely? What a dangerous train
>   Did he give fire to! How he shook the king,
>   Made his soul melt within him, and his blood
>   Run into whey! It stood upon his brow 295
>   Like a cold winter dew.

PHILASTER.   Gentlemen,
>   You have no suit to me? I am no minion.
>   You stand methinks like men that would be courtiers
>   If you could well be flatter'd at a price
>   Not to undo your children. Y'are all honest. 300

---

284. *hot at hand*] Daniel cites the phrase "like horses hot at hand" in *Julius Caesar*, IV.ii.23. G. B. Harrison *(Shakespeare, the Complete Works,* 1952 ed.) glosses *hot at hand* as meaning horses which are restless when the rider wishes them to stand.

287. *home things*] things that strike home; effective actions or words.

289. *head-piece*] covering for the head; here, probably the head itself.

290. *night cap*] possible reference to a horse's nightcap, or halter *(OED)*; Megra's weak head needs the restraint of a halter. *Night cap* may also suggest "bed companion."

295. *whey*] "the serum of the blood" *(OED)*; here, perspiration.

297. *minion*] favorite of a sovereign, often used contemptuously to denote a servile creature *(OED)*.

299. *you*] so all early editions; emended by Weber (Mason's suggestion) and later editors except Turner to "I." Mason, quoted by Weber, conjectures that the meaning is, "You look as if you could be willing to pay your court to me, if you could do so without hazarding the fortunes of your families by offending the king." Turner retains *you,* paraphrasing Philaster thus: "You are dancing attendance upon me like courtiers, as if you could be flattered (pleased) for a price not to undo your own children."

I.i PHILASTER

Go, get you home again and make your country
A virtuous court to which your great ones may
In their diseased age retire and live recluse.
CLEREMONT.
How do you, worthy sir?
PHILASTER. Well, very well.
And so well that, if the king please, I find 305
I may live many years.
DION. The king must please,
Whilst we know what you are and who you are,
Your wrongs and injuries. Shrink not, worthy sir,
But add your father to you, in whose name
We'll waken all the gods and conjure up 310
The rods of vengeance, the abused people
Who like to raging torrents shall swell high
And so begirt the dens of these male dragons
That through the strongest safety they shall beg
For mercy at your sword's point.
PHILASTER. Friends, no more. 315
Our ears may be corrupted. 'Tis an age
We dare not trust our wills to. Do you love me?
THRASILINE.
Do we love heaven and honor?
PHILASTER. My lord Dion, you had
A virtuous gentlewoman call'd you father.
Is she yet alive?
DION. Most honor'd sir, she is, 320
And for the penance but of an idle dream
Has undertook a tedious pilgrimage.

Enter a Lady.

PHILASTER.
Is it to me or any of these gentlemen you come?
LADY.
To you, brave lord. The princess would entreat
Your present company. 325

---

313. *male dragons*] masculine; possibly evil (Dyce).
322. *Has . . . pilgrimage*] Journeys to religious shrines were sometimes undertaken in atonement for a sin or personal shortcoming.

—18—

PHILASTER.
    The princess send for me? Y'are mistaken.
LADY.
    If you be call'd Philaster, 'tis to you.
PHILASTER.
    Kiss her fair hand and say I will attend her.
                                              [*Exit* Lady.]
DION.
    Do you know what you do?
PHILASTER.
    Yes, go to see a woman.   330
CLEREMONT.
    But do you weigh the danger you are in?
PHILASTER.
    Danger in a sweet face?
    By Jupiter I must not fear a woman.
THRASILINE.
    But are you sure it was the princess sent?
    It may be some foul train to catch your life.   335
PHILASTER.
    I do not think it, gentlemen. She's noble.
    Her eye may shoot me dead, or those true red
    And white friends in her face may steal my soul out.
    There's all the danger in't. But be what may,
    Her single name hath arm'd me.   *Exit* Philaster. 340
DION.
    Go on, and be as truly happy as thou'rt fearless.
    Come, gentlemen, let's make our friends acquainted
    Lest the king prove false.   *Exeunt* Gentlemen.

[I.ii]   *Enter* Arethusa *and a* Lady.

ARETHUSA.
    Comes he not?
LADY.   Madam?

---

335. *train*] "lure, false device" (Onions); originally a trap or snare for catching wild animals *(OED)*.
340. *Her single name*] her name alone.

I.ii   PHILASTER

ARETHUSA.   Will Philaster come?
LADY.
    Dear madam, you were wont
    To credit me at first.
ARETHUSA.
    But didst thou tell me so?
    I am forgetful, and my woman's strength 5
    Is so o'ercharged with dangers like to grow
    About my marriage that these under-things
    Dare not abide in such a troubled sea.
    How look'd he when he told thee he would come?
LADY.
    Why, well. 10
ARETHUSA.
    And not a little fearful?
LADY.
    Fear, madam? Sure he knows not what it is.
ARETHUSA.
    You all are of his faction. The whole court
    Is bold in praise of him, whilst I
    May live neglected and do noble things 15
    As fools in strife throw gold into the sea,
    Drown'd in the doing. But I know he fears.
LADY.
    Fear? Madam, methought his looks hid more
    Of love than fear.
ARETHUSA.   Of love? To whom? To you?
    Did you deliver those plain words I sent 20
    With such a winning gesture and quick look
    That you have caught him?
LADY.   Madam, I mean to you.
ARETHUSA.
    Of love to me? Alas, thy ignorance
    Lets thee not see the crosses of our births.
    Nature, that loves not to be questioned 25

---

    7. *under-things*] lower or inferior things *(OED;* the only illustrative quotation is this passage).
    21. *quick*] lively (Dyce).
    24. *crosses*] "a crossing or thwarting" *(OED).*

	PHILASTER	I.ii

<blockquote>

Why she did this or that but has her ends
And knows she does well, never gave the world
Two things so opposite, so contrary,
As he and I am. If a bowl of blood
Drawn from this arm of mine would poison thee, 30
A draught of his would cure thee. Of love to me!
</blockquote>

LADY.
> Madam, I think I hear him.

ARETHUSA. Bring him in. [*Exit* Lady.]
> You gods that would not have your dooms withstood,
> Whose holy wisdoms at this time it is
> To make the passions of a feeble maid 35
> The way unto your justice, I obey.

Enter [Lady *with*] Philaster.

LADY.
> Here is my lord Philaster.

ARETHUSA. Oh, it is well.
> Withdraw yourself. [*Exit* Lady.]

PHILASTER. Madam, your messenger
> Made me believe you wish'd to speak with me.

ARETHUSA.
> 'Tis true, Philaster, but the words are such 40
> I have to say, and do so ill beseem
> The mouth of woman, that I wish them said
> And yet am loath to speak them. Have you known
> That I have aught detracted from your worth?
> Have I in person wrong'd you, or have set 45
> My baser instruments to throw disgrace
> Upon your virtues?

PHILASTER. Never, madam, you.

ARETHUSA.
> Why then should you in such a public place
> Injure a princess and a scandal lay
> Upon my fortunes, fam'd to be so great, 50
> Calling a great part of my dowry in question?

---

33. *dooms*] judgments.
46. *baser instruments*] servants, attendants.
50. *fam'd*] rumored, reported.

I.ii   PHILASTER

PHILASTER.
    Madam, this truth which I shall speak will be
    Foolish. But for your fair and virtuous self
    I could afford myself to have no right
    To anything you wish'd.
ARETHUSA.   Philaster, know   55
    I must enjoy these kingdoms.
PHILASTER.   Madam, both?
ARETHUSA.
    Both, or I die. By heaven, I die, Philaster,
    If I not calmly may enjoy them both.
PHILASTER.
    I would do much to save that noble life,
    Yet would be loath to have posterity   60
    Find in our stories that Philaster gave
    His right unto a scepter and a crown
    To save a lady's longing.
ARETHUSA.   Nay then, hear:
    I must and will have them, and more.
PHILASTER.   What more?
ARETHUSA.
    Or lose that little life the gods prepar'd   65
    To trouble this poor piece of earth withal.
PHILASTER.
    Madam, what more?
ARETHUSA.   Turn then away thy face.
PHILASTER.
    No.
ARETHUSA.
    Do.
PHILASTER.
    I can endure it. Turn away my face?   70
    I never yet saw enemy that look'd
    So dreadfully but that I thought myself

---

54. *afford*] "manage to give, to spare; grant, yield" *(OED)*.
58. *calmly*] peacefully, serenely.

As great a basilisk as he, or spake
So horrible but that I thought my tongue
Bore thunder underneath as much as his, 75
Nor beast that I could turn from. Shall I then
Begin to fear sweet sounds? A lady's voice
Whom I do love? Say you would have my life;
Why, I will give it you. For it is of me
A thing so loath'd, and unto you that ask 80
Of so poor use, that I shall make no price.
If you entreat, I will unmov'dly hear.
ARETHUSA.
Yet for my sake a little bend thy looks.
PHILASTER.
I do.
ARETHUSA. Then know I must have them and thee.
PHILASTER.
And me?
ARETHUSA. Thy love, without which all the land 85
Discover'd yet will serve me for no use
But to be buried in.
PHILASTER. Is't possible?
ARETHUSA.
With it, it were too little to bestow
On thee. Now, though thy breath do strike me dead
(Which know it may), I have unripp'd my breast. 90
PHILASTER.
Madam, you are too full of noble thoughts
To lay a train for this contemned life
Which you may have for asking. To suspect
Were base, where I deserve no ill. Love you?
By all my hopes I do, above my life! 95
But how this passion should proceed from you
So violently would amaze a man
That would be jealous.

---

73. *basilisk*] "fabulous reptile, also called cockatrice, supposed to be hatched by a serpent from a cock's egg and said to kill by its breath and look" (Onions).

83. *bend*] "inclination of the eye in any direction, glance" *(OED)*.

92. *contemned*] despised.

98. *jealous*] suspicious, doubtful, mistrustful (Onions).

I.ii   PHILASTER

ARETHUSA.
    Another soul into my body shot
    Could not have fill'd me with more strength and spirit 100
    Than this thy breath. But spend not hasty time
    In seeking how I came thus. 'Tis the gods,
    The gods that make me so. And sure our love
    Will be the nobler and the better blest
    In that the secret justice of the gods 105
    Is mingled with it. Let us leave and kiss,
    Lest some unwelcome guest should fall betwixt us
    And we should part without it.
PHILASTER.   'Twill be ill
    I should abide here long.
ARETHUSA.   'Tis true, and worse
    You should come often. How shall we devise 110
    To hold intelligence, that our true loves
    On any new occasion may agree
    What path is best to tread?
PHILASTER.   I have a boy
    Sent by the gods, I hope, to this intent,
    Not yet seen in the court. Hunting the buck, 115
    I found him sitting by a fountain's side,
    Of which he borrowed some to quench his thirst
    And paid the nymph again as much in tears.
    A garland lay him by, made by himself
    Of many several flowers bred in the bay, 120

---

    101. *hasty*] fleeting.
    106. *leave*] "cease, desist from, stop" *(OED)*; here, to cease discussing.
    116. *sitting . . . side*] possibly an allusion to the sacred fountain Arethusa in Sicily, whose story is told by Ovid in *Metamorphoses* 5. 572-641; the *nymph* of l. 118 would be the goddess Arethusa herself, one of Diana's retinue who was turned into a fountain to escape the pursuit of the river god Alpheus.
    118. *nymph*] in mythology, a semi-divine maiden often inhabiting streams or rustic settings.
    120. *several*] different.
    120. *bred in the bay*] so Q2-9 and F, followed by Turner. Dyce accepts the Q1 reading, *bred in the vale*. Mason, quoted by Weber, conjectures that the Q2 reading means "woven (embroidered, brede) into the garland (bay)." Weber suggests that the meaning is simply

PHILASTER   I.ii

Stuck in that mystic order that the rareness
Delighted me. But ever when he turn'd
His tender eyes upon 'em, he would weep
As if he meant to make 'em grow again.
Seeing such pretty helpless innocence   125
Dwell in his face, I ask'd him all his story.
He told me that his parents gentle died,
Leaving him to the mercy of the fields
Which gave him roots, and of the crystal springs
Which did not stop their courses, and the sun   130
Which still, he thank'd him, yielded him his light.
Then took he up his garland and did show
What every flower, as country people hold,
Did signify and how all ordered thus
Express'd his grief; and to my thoughts did read   135
The prettiest lecture of his country art
That could be wish'd, so that methought I could
Have studied it. I gladly entertain'd him
Who was glad to follow and have got
The trustiest, loving'st, and the gentlest boy   140
That ever master kept. Him will I send
To wait on you and bear our hidden love.

ARETHUSA.
'Tis well. No more.

Enter Lady.

LADY.
Madam, the prince is come to do his service.

"bred (grown) on the shallow edge of the fountain." Another possibility is that *bay* could be meant in the obsolete sense of "an indentation or rounded projection of the land into the sea" *(OED,* citing a passage of 1611); also an indentation or recess in a range of hills *(OED,* 1853 passage: "The hills . . . stand out generally well-defined by bays and vales, which run in about their bases"). Turner cites a use of bay as "any bank across a stream."

121. *that mystic order*] Both the arrangement of flowers and the flowers themselves (cf. ll. 133–134 below: *What every flower . . ./ Did signify)* had symbolic significance to the Elizabethans, as in Ophelia's speech *(Hamlet,* IV.v.175 ff.): "There's rosemary, that's for remembrance . . . ."

144. *service*] attention of a gallant to his lady.

I.ii   PHILASTER

ARETHUSA.
    What will you do, Philaster, with yourself?   145
PHILASTER.
    Why, that which all the gods have appointed out for me.
ARETHUSA.
    Dear, hide thyself. [*To* Lady.] Bring in the prince.
                                                                [*Exit* Lady.]
PHILASTER.
    Hide me from Pharamond?
    When thunder speaks, which is the voice of God,
    Though I do reverence, yet I hide me not.   150
    And shall a stranger prince have leave to brag
    Unto a foreign nation that he made
    Philaster hide himself?
ARETHUSA.   He cannot know it.
PHILASTER.
    Though it should sleep forever to the world,
    It is a simple sin to hide myself   155
    Which will forever on my conscience lie.
ARETHUSA.
    Then, good Philaster, give him scope and way
    In what he says, for he is apt to speak
    What you are loath to hear. For my sake, do.
PHILASTER.
    I will.   160
                    Enter Pharamond.
PHARAMOND.
    My princely mistress, as true lovers ought
    I come to kiss these fair hands and to show
    In outward ceremonies the dear love
    Writ in my heart.
PHILASTER.
    If I shall have an answer no directlier,   165
    I am gone.

---

  146. *appointed*] "to determine authoritatively, prescribe, decree, ordain"; also used in the sense of "pointed out" *(OED)*. Weber, followed by Dyce and other editors (not Turner), emends to "pointed out."

  155. *simple*] mere, pure, bare *(OED)*; plain (Onions).

  160.1] Dyce emends to "*Re-enter* Lady *with* Pharamond."

PHARAMOND. To what would he have answer?
ARETHUSA.
 To his claim unto the kingdom.
PHARAMOND.
 Sirrah, I forbear you before the king.
PHILASTER.
 Good sir, do so still. I would not talk with you.
PHARAMOND.
 But now the time is fitter. Do but offer 170
 To make mention of right to any kingdom,
 Though it lie scarce habitable—
PHILASTER.
 Good sir, let me go.
PHARAMOND.
 And by the gods—
PHILASTER.
 Peace, Pharamond. If thou— 175
ARETHUSA.
 Leave us, Philaster.
PHILASTER.
 I have gone.
PHARAMOND.
 You are gone! By heaven, I'll fetch you back!
PHILASTER.
 You shall not need.
PHARAMOND.   What now?
PHILASTER.   Know, Pharamond,
 I loathe to brawl with such a blast as thou 180
 Who art nought but a valiant voice. But if
 Thou shalt provoke me further, men shall say
 Thou wert, and not lament it.
PHARAMOND.   Do you slight
 My greatness so, and in the chamber of the princess?
PHILASTER.
 It is a place to which, I must confess, 185
 I owe a reverence, but were't the church,

---

168. *forbear*] tolerated, indulged.
180. *blast*] boaster, vaunter.

   Ay, at the altar, there's no place so safe
   Where thou dar'st injure me but I dare kill thee.
   And for your greatness know, sir, I can grasp
   You and your greatness thus, thus, into nothing!   190
   Give not a word, not a word back. Farewell.   *Exit.*

PHARAMOND.
   'Tis an odd fellow, madam. We must stop
   His mouth with some office when we are married.

ARETHUSA.
   You were best make him your controller.

PHARAMOND.
   I think he would discharge it well. But madam,   195
   I hope our hearts are knit, but yet so slow
   The ceremonies of state are that 'twill be long
   Before our hands be so. If then you please,
   Being agreed in heart, let us not wait
   For dreaming form but take a little stolen   200
   Delights and so prevent our joys to come.

ARETHUSA.
   If you dare speak such thoughts
   I must withdraw in honor.   *Exit* Arethusa.

PHARAMOND.
   The constitution of my body will never hold out till the
   wedding. I must seek elsewhere.   *Exit* Pharamond. 205

[II.i]   *Enter* Philaster *and* Bellario.

PHILASTER.
   And thou shalt find her honorable, boy,
   Full of regard unto thy tender youth;
   For thine own modesty, and for my sake,
   Apter to give than thou wilt be to ask,
   Ay, or deserve.

BELLARIO.   Sir, you did take me up   5

---

 194. *controller*] comptroller, official who checks expenditures; here used ironically.
 201. *prevent*] anticipate.
[II.i]
 5-10. *Ay . . . boy*] Verse has been relined as in Theobald, Dyce.

When I was nothing, and only yet am something
By being yours. You trusted me unknown,
And that which you were apt to conster
A simple innocence in me, perhaps
Might have been craft, the cunning of a boy   10
Harden'd in lies and theft. Yet ventur'd you
To part my miseries and me, for which
I never can expect to serve a lady
That bears more honor in her breast than you.
PHILASTER.
But, boy, it will prefer thee. Thou art young   15
And bearest a childish overflowing love
To them that clap thy cheeks and speak thee fair yet.
But when thy judgment comes to rule those passions,
Thou wilt remember best those careful friends
That plac'd thee in the noblest way of life.   20
She is a princess I prefer thee to.
BELLARIO.
In that small time that I have seen the world,
I never knew a man hasty to part
With a servant he thought trusty. I remember
My father would prefer the boys he kept   25
To greater men than he, but did it not
Till they were grown too saucy for himself.
PHILASTER.
Why, gentle boy, I find no fault at all
In thy behavior.
BELLARIO.   Sir, if I have made
A fault of ignorance, instruct my youth.   30
I shall be willing if not apt to learn.
Age and experience will adorn my mind
With larger knowledge; and if I have done
A wilful fault, think me not past all hope
For once. What master holds so strict a hand   35

---

8. *conster*] construe.

15. *prefer*] "put forward or advance, in status, rank, or fortune" *(OED)*.

21. *prefer*] in the general sense of "put forward"; also "refer" *(OED)*.

II.i   PHILASTER

    Over his boy that he will part with him
    Without one warning? Let me be corrected
    To break my stubbornness, if it be so,
    Rather than turn me off, and I shall mend.

PHILASTER.
    Thy love doth plead so prettily to stay   40
    That, trust me, I could weep to part with thee.
    Alas, I do not turn thee off. Thou knowest
    It is my business that doth call thee hence,
    And when thou art with her thou dwellest with me.
    Think so and 'tis so. And when time is full   45
    That thou hast well discharg'd this heavy trust
    Laid on so weak a one, I will again
    With joy receive thee. As I live I will!
    Nay, weep not, gentle boy. 'Tis more than time
    Thou didst attend the princess.

BELLARIO.   I am gone.   50
    But since I am to part with you, my lord,
    And none knows whether I shall live to do
    More service for you, take this little prayer:
    Heaven bless your loves, your fights, all your designs;
    May sick men, if they have your wish, be well;   **55**
    And heaven hate those you curse, though I be one.   *Exit.*

PHILASTER.
    The love of boys unto their lords is strange.
    I have read wonders of it; yet this boy
    For my sake, if a man may judge by looks
    And speech, would outdo story. I may see   60
    A day to pay him for his loyalty.   *Exit* Philaster.

[II.ii]   *Enter* Pharamond.

PHARAMOND.
    Why should these ladies stay so long? They must come
    this way. I know the queen employs 'em not, for the
    reverend mother sent me word they would all be for the

---

    3. *reverend mother*] the Mother of the Maids (Dyce); the woman who chaperones and supervises the ladies-in-waiting at court.

garden. If they should all prove honest now, I were in
a fair taking. I was never so long without sport in my
life, and in my conscience 'tis not my fault. Oh, for our
country ladies!

Enter Galatea.

Here's one bolted; I'll hound at her. Madam!
GALATEA.
Your grace.
PHARAMOND.
Shall I not be a trouble?
GALATEA.
Not to me, sir.
PHARAMOND.
Nay, nay, you are too quick. By this sweet hand—
GALATEA.
You'll be forsworn, sir. 'Tis but an old glove. If you
will talk at distance, I am for you. But, good prince, be
not bawdy nor do not brag. These two I bar, and then I
think I shall have sense enough to answer all the weighty
apothegms your royal blood shall manage.
PHARAMOND.
Dear lady, can you love?
GALATEA.
Dear prince, how dear? I ne'er cost you a coach yet nor
put you to the dear repentance of a banquet. Here's no
scarlet, sir, to blush the sin out it was given for. This

---

4. *honest*] chaste (Dyce).

8. *bolted*] "to rush suddenly off or away" *(OED,* citing this passage).

8. *hound*] pursue, set on, as hunting dogs in a chase.

8. *Madam*] Q1 followed by Dyce and later editors; omitted in other early editions. Turner conjectures that the word was accidentally omitted by the Q2 compositor, who then added it as a proof correction in the wrong place (1. 111 of the present edition). Hence Turner omits *Madam* in the latter passage, as do most modern editors and all early texts except Q2, 3, and 9.

13. *forsworn*] perjured; falsely sworn.

17. *apothegms*] precepts, maxims.

21. *scarlet*] scarlet-colored cloth or clothes; implied meaning of whorish.

II.ii   PHILASTER

wire mine own hair covers, and this face has been so far
from being dear to any that it ne'er cost penny painting.
And for the rest of my poor wardrobe, such as you see,
it leaves no hand behind it to make the jealous mercer's   25
wife curse our good doings.

PHARAMOND.
You mistake me, lady.

GALATEA.
Lord, I do so. Would you or I could help it!

PHARAMOND.
Do ladies of this country use to give no more respect to
men of my full being?   30

GALATEA.
Full being? I understand you not, unless your grace
means growing to fatness, and then your only remedy,
upon my knowledge, prince, is in a morning a cup of
neat white wine brew'd with carduus, then fast till sup-
per. About eight you may eat. Use exercise and keep   35
a sparrow hawk; you can shoot in a tiller. But of all
your grace must fly phlebotomy, fresh pork, conger, and
clarified whey. They are all dullers of the vital spirits.

PHARAMOND.
Lady, you talk of nothing all this while.

---

22. *wire*] a frame of wire to support the hair or ruff *(OED)*; at times a formal cap with a wire framework.

25. *no . . . it*] no indebtedness remaining on the tradesman's books (Daniel).

25. *mercer's*] silk-merchant's; one who deals in textile fabrics *(OED)*.

28. *Lord . . . it*] Q1 adds two speeches after this line, incorporated into the text by Dyce and later editors: "*Pharamond*. Y'are very dangerous bitter, like a potion. *Galatea*. No, sir, I do not mean to purge you, though I mean to purge a little time on you."

34. *neat*] undiluted.

34. *carduus*] "Carduus Benedictus, the Blessed Thistle, noted for its medicinal properties" (Onions).

36. *tiller*] "a stock or shaft fixed to a long-bow to admit of its being used as a cross-bow, for greater convenience or precision of aim" *(OED,* citing this passage).

37. *phlebotomy*] medical treatment by bloodletting.

37. *conger*] a large species of salt-water eel, used for food *(OED)*.

38. *clarified whey*] the watery part of milk, left standing to clear.

PHILASTER II.ii

GALATEA.
'Tis very true, sir; I talk of you. 40
PHARAMOND.
This is a crafty wench. I like her wit well; 'twill be rare to stir up a leaden appetite. She's a Danaë and must be courted in a shower of gold. Madam, look here. All these and more than—
GALATEA.
What have you there, my lord? Gold? Now, as I live, 45 'tis fair gold. You would have silver for it to play with the pages. You could not have taken me in a worse time, but if you have present use, my lord, I'll send my man with silver and keep your gold for you.
PHARAMOND.
Lady, lady! 50
GALATEA.
She's coming, sir, behind will take white money. Yet for all this I'll match ye. *Exit* Galatea *behind the hangings.*
PHARAMOND.
If there be but two such more in this kingdom and near the court, we may even hang up our harps. Ten such camphor constitutions as this would call the golden age 55 again in question, and teach the old way for every ill-fac'd husband to get his own children. And what a mischief that will breed, let all consider.

---

42. *Danaë*] the mother of Perseus by Zeus, who visited her as a shower of gold in her prison tower.

51. *white money*] "cant name for silver specie" (Dyce).

54. *hang up our harps*] give up the enterprise; *The Oxford Dictionary of English Proverbs* (1948) notes "hang one's harp on the willows," as in Smollett's *Reprisal* (1757), I.8: "All our fine project gone to pot! — We may now hang up our harps among the willows."

55. *camphor*] cold, frigid; camphor was "formerly in repute as an antaphrodisiac"; as in Dryden's *Spanish Fryar* (1681), V.149, "Prescribe her an Ounce of Camphire every Morning . . . to abate Incontinency" *(OED)*.

55. *golden age*] in classical mythology, a period of perfect peace and happiness.

II.ii   PHILASTER

                        Enter Megra.

Here's another. If she be of the same last, the devil shall
plauck her on. Many fair mornings, lady!   60
MEGRA.
  As many mornings bring as many days
  Fair, sweet, and hopeful to your grace.
PHARAMOND [*aside*].
  She gives good words yet. Sure this wench is free.—
  If your more serious business do not call you,
  Let me hold quarter with you. We'll talk an hour   65
  Out quickly.
MEGRA.   What would your grace talk of?
PHARAMOND.
  Of some such pretty subject as yourself.
  I'll go no further than your eye or lip.
  There's theme enough for one man for an age.
MEGRA.
  Sir, they stand right, and my lips are yet even,   70
  Smooth, young enough, ripe enough, and red enough,
  Or my glass wrongs me.
PHARAMOND.
  Oh, they are two twinn'd cherries dyed in blushes
  Which those fair suns above with their bright beams
  Reflect upon and ripen. Sweetest beauty,   75
  Bow down those branches that the longing taste
  Of the faint looker-on may meet those blessings
  And taste and live.
MEGRA [*aside*].   Oh, delicate sweet prince,
  She that hath snow enough about her heart
  To take the wanton spring of ten such lines off   80
  May be a nun without probation.—

---

59. *last*] shoemaker's wooden model of the foot, used to shape footwear *(OED)*.

59–60. *the devil . . . on*] equivalent to "the devil take her!"

65. *hold quarter with*] "to remain beside" *(OED,* citing this passage); to converse in a friendly way.

81. *probation*] "testing or trial of a person's conduct, character, or moral qualifications," as of a candidate for holy orders or for membership in a religious body *(OED,* citing this passage).

—34—

II.ii

Sir, you have in such neat poetry gather'd a kiss
That if I had but five lines of that number,
Such pretty begging blanks, I should commend
Your forehead or your cheeks and kiss you, too.   85
PHARAMOND.
Do it in prose. You cannot miss it, madam.
MEGRA.
I shall, I shall.
PHARAMOND.   By my life, you shall not.
I'll prompt you first. [*Kisses her.*] Can you do it now?
MEGRA.
Methinks 'tis easy now I ha' done't before,
But yet I should stick at it.
PHARAMOND.   Stick till tomorrow;   90
I'll ne'er part you, sweetest. But we lose time.
Can you love me?
MEGRA.
Love you, my lord? How would you have me love you?
PHARAMOND.
I'll teach you in a short sentence 'cause I will not load
your memory. This is all: love me and lie with me.   95
MEGRA.
Was it lie with you that you said? 'Tis impossible.
PHARAMOND.
Not to a willing mind that will endeavor. If I do not
teach you to do it as easily in one night as you'll go to
bed, I'll lose my royal blood for't.
MEGRA.
Why, prince, you have a lady of your own that yet wants 100
teaching.
PHARAMOND.
I'll sooner teach a mare the old measures than teach her
anything belonging to the function. She's afraid to lie
with herself if she have but any masculine imaginations
about her. I know when we are married I must ravish 105
her.

---

84. *blanks*] blank verses (Dyce).
100. *wants*] lacks, needs.

II.ii   PHILASTER

MEGRA.

By mine honor, that's a foul fault indeed, but time and your good help will wear it out, sir.

PHARAMOND.

And for any other I see, excepting your dear self, dearest lady, I had rather be Sir Tim the schoolmaster and leap 110 a dairy maid. Madam!

MEGRA.

Has your grace seen the court star, Galatea?

PHARAMOND.

Out upon her! She's as cold of her favor as an apoplex. She sail'd by but now.

MEGRA.

And how do you hold her wit, sir? 115

PHARAMOND.

I hold her wit? The strength of all the guard cannot hold it, if they were tied to it; she would blow 'em out of the kingdom. They talk of Jupiter; he's but a squib-cracker to her. Look well about you and you may find a tongue bolt. But speak, sweet lady; shall I be freely 120 welcome?

MEGRA.

Whither?

PHARAMOND.

To your bed. If you mistrust my faith, you do me the unnoblest wrong.

---

110. *Sir Tim the schoolmaster*] "Tim" in the seventeenth century was a term of personal abuse, as in Jonson's *Alchemist* (1610), IV.vii: "Then you are an Otter, and a Shad, a Whit, a very Tim" *(OED)*.

113. *apoplex*] stroke; apoplexy.

118–119. *squibcracker*] firecracker.

120. *tongue bolt*] *OED* cites many uses, including this one, of phrases like "tongue-banger," "tongue-batteries," "tongue-bolts," as in R. A. Vaughan's *Mystics* (1856), "The . . . doctors of Lyons hurled back his tongue-bolts with the dreaded cry of heresy." In contrast with Jupiter's thunderbolts, Galatea throws fiery words with her tongue. Here her conduct is reminiscent of that of her mythological namesake Galatea, who mocked her lover Polyphemus until he lamented that he feared her angry tongue more than the thunderbolts of Jove (Ovid's *Metamorphoses* 2. 738–897).

MEGRA.
   I dare not, prince, I dare not. 125
PHARAMOND.
   Make your own conditions, my purse shall seal 'em; and what you dare imagine you can want, I'll furnish you withal. Give two hours to your thoughts every morning about it. Come, I know you are bashful. Speak in my ear. Will you be mine? Keep this, and with it me. Soon 130 I will visit you.
MEGRA.
   My lord, my chamber's most unsafe, but when 'tis night I'll find some means to slip into your lodging; till when—
PHARAMOND.
   Till when, this and my heart go with thee. *Exeunt.*

   Enter Galatea *from behind the hangings.*

GALATEA.
   Oh, thou pernicious petticoat prince, are these your 135 virtues? Well, if I do not lay a train to blow your sport up, I am no woman. And, Lady Towsabell, I'll fit you for't. *Exit* Galatea.

[II.iii]   *Enter* Arethusa *and a* Lady.

ARETHUSA.
   Where's the boy?
LADY.
   Within, madam.
ARETHUSA.
   Gave you him gold to buy him clothes?
LADY.
   I did.
ARETHUSA.
   And has he done't? 5

---

130. *Keep this*] Weber, followed by Dyce, Daniel, and others, adds the stage direction *"Gives her a ring";* Turner adds *"Gives her money."*
137. *Towsabell*] "a jocular alteration of Dowsabell, which is a name common in our early pastoral poetry" (Dyce).

II.iii   PHILASTER

LADY.
> Yes, madam.

ARETHUSA.
> 'Tis a pretty sad-talking boy, is it not? Ask'd you his name?

LADY.
> No, madam.

Enter Galatea.

ARETHUSA.
> Oh, you are welcome. What good news?   10

GALATEA.
> As good as anyone can tell your grace that says, she has done that you would have wish'd.

ARETHUSA.
> Hast thou discover'd?

GALATEA.
> I have strain'd a point of modesty for you.

ARETHUSA.
> I pray thee, how?   15

GALATEA.
> In list'ning after bawdry. I see, let a lady live never so modestly, she shall be sure to find a lawful time to harken after bawdry. Your prince, brave Pharamond, was so hot on't.

ARETHUSA.
> With whom?   20

GALATEA.
> Why, with the lady I suspected. I can tell you the time and place.

ARETHUSA.
> Oh, when and where?

GALATEA.
> Tonight, his lodging.

ARETHUSA.
> Run thyself into the presence, mingle there again   25
> With other ladies. Leave the rest to me.   [*Exit* Galatea.]

---

13. *discover'd*] come to the knowledge of, find out *(OED)*.

If destiny, to whom we dare not say
Why thou didst this, have not decreed it so
In lasting leaves whose smallest characters
Was never alter'd yet, this match shall break. 30
Where's the boy?

Enter Bellario.

LADY.
Here, madam.
ARETHUSA.
Sir, you are sad to change your service, is't not so?
BELLARIO.
Madam, I have not chang'd. I wait on you
To do him service.
ARETHUSA.   Thou disclaim'st in me. 35
Tell me your name.
BELLARIO.   Bellario.
ARETHUSA.
Thou canst sing and play?
BELLARIO.
If grief will give me leave, madam, I can.
ARETHUSA.
Alas, what kind of grief can thy years know?
Hadst thou a curst master when thou went'st to school? 40
Thou art not capable of other grief.
Thy brows and cheeks are smooth as waters be
When no breath troubles them. Believe me, boy,
Care seeks out wrinkled brows and hollow eyes,
And builds himself caves to abide in them. 45
Come, sir, tell me truly, doth your lord love me?
BELLARIO.
Love, madam? I know not what it is.
ARETHUSA.
Canst thou know grief and never yet knew'st love?

---

29. *leaves*] pages in the book of destiny or fate.
29. *characters*] letters.
31. *Enter Bellario*] Dyce adds *"richly dressed."*
35. *disclaim'st in me*] meaning "disclaim'st me" (Dyce).
40. *curst*] "perversely disagreeable or cross" *(OED)*.

II.iii   PHILASTER

    Thou art deceived, boy. Does he speak of me
    As if he wish'd me well?
BELLARIO.   If it be love   50
    To forget all respect to his own friends
    With thinking of your face; if it be love
    To sit cross-arm'd and think away the day
    Mingled with starts, crying your name as loud
    And hastily as men i'the streets do fire;   55
    If it be love to weep himself away
    When he but hears of any lady dead
    Or kill'd because it might have been your chance;
    If when he goes to rest (which will not be),
    'Twixt every prayer he says to name you once   60
    As others drop a bead, be to be in love;
    Then, madam, I dare swear he loves you.
ARETHUSA.
    Oh, y'are a cunning boy and taught to lie
    For your lord's credit. But thou know'st a lie
    That bears this sound is welcomer to me   65
    Than any truth that says he loves me not.
    Lead the way, boy. [*To* Lady.] Do you attend me, too.
    'Tis thy lord's business hastes me thus. Away!   *Exeunt.*

[II.iv] *Enter* Dion, Cleremont, Thrasiline, Megra, Galatea.

DION.
    Come, ladies, shall we talk a round? As men
    Do walk a mile, women should talk an hour
    After supper. 'Tis their exercise.
GALATEA.
    'Tis late.
MEGRA.
    'Tis all my eyes will do to lead me to my bed.   5
GALATEA.
    I fear they are so heavy thee'll scarce find
    The way to your own lodging with 'em tonight.

                Enter Pharamond.
THRASILINE.
    The prince!

PHARAMOND.
> Not abed, ladies? Y'are good sitters up.
> What think you of a pleasant dream to last till morning? 10

MEGRA.
> I should choose, my lord, a pleasing wake before it.

Enter Arethusa *and* Bellario.

ARETHUSA.
> 'Tis well, my lord. Y'are courting of these ladies.
> Is't not late, gentlemen?

CLEREMONT.
> Yes, madam.

ARETHUSA.
> Wait you there.   *Exit* Arethusa. 15

MEGRA.
> She's jealous, as I live. Look you, my lord,
> The princess has a Hylas, an Adonis.

PHARAMOND.
> His form is angel-like.

MEGRA.
> Why, this is he must, when you are wed,
> Sit by your pillow like young Apollo with   20
> His hand and voice binding your thoughts in sleep.
> The princess does provide him for you, and for herself.

PHARAMOND.
> I find no music in these boys.

MEGRA.   Nor I.
> They can do little, and that small they do
> They have not wit to hide.

DION.   Serves he the princess?

THRASILINE.   Yes. 25

DION.
> 'Tis a sweet boy. How brave she keeps him!

---

17. *Hylas*] young armor-bearer to Hercules.
17. *Adonis*] beautiful youth loved by Aphrodite.
20. *Apollo*] Greek god, also called Phoebus.
26. *brave*] "finely-dressed . . . splendid, showy" *(OED)*.

II.iv   PHILASTER

PHARAMOND.
> Ladies all, good rest. I mean to kill a buck
> Tomorrow morning ere y'have done your dreams.

MEGRA.
> All happiness attend your grace.   [*Exit* Pharamond.]
> Gentlemen, good rest. Come, shall we to bed?   30

GALATEA.
> Yes, all good night.   *Exeunt* Galatea, Megra.

DION.
> May your dreams be true to you.
> What shall we do, gallants? 'Tis late. The king
> Is up still; see, he comes, a guard along
> With him.   35

Enter King, Arethusa, *and guard.*

KING.
> Look your intelligence be true.

ARETHUSA.
> Upon my life it is, and I do hope
> Your highness will not tie me to a man
> That in the heat of wooing throws me off
> And takes another.   40

DION.
> What should this mean?

KING.
> If it be true,
> That lady had been better have embrac'd
> Cureless diseases. Get you to your rest;
> You shall be righted.   *Exeunt* Arethusa, Bellario.
>   Gentlemen, draw near.   45
> We shall employ you. Is young Pharamond
> Come to his lodging?

DION.   I saw him enter there.

KING.
> Haste, some of you, and cunningly discover
> If Megra be in her lodging.   [*Exit* Dion.]

CLEREMONT.
> Sir, she parted hence but now with other ladies.   50

---

36. *intelligence*] information.

KING.
> If she be there, we shall not need to make
> A vain discovery of our suspicion.
> [*Aside.*] You gods, I see that who unrighteously
> Holds wealth or state from others shall be curst
> In that which meaner men are blest withal. 55
> Ages to come shall know no male of him
> Left to inherit, and his name shall be
> Blotted from earth. If he have any child,
> It shall be crossly match'd. The gods themselves
> Shall sow wild strife betwixt her lord and her. 60
> Yet if it be your wills, forgive the sin
> I have committed. Let it not fall
> Upon this understanding child of mine;
> She has not broke your laws. But how can I
> Look to be heard of gods that must be just, 65
> Praying upon the ground I hold by wrong?

Enter Dion.

DION.
> Sir, I have ask'd and her women swear she is within, but they I think are bawds. I told 'em I must speak with her. They laugh'd and said their lady lay speechless. I said my business was important; they said their 70 lady was about it. I grew hot and cried, my business was a matter that concern'd life and death. They answer'd, so was sleeping, at which their lady was. I urg'd again she had scarce time to be so since last I saw her. They smil'd again and seem'd to instruct me that sleeping was 75 nothing but lying down and winking. Answers more direct I could not get. In short, sir, I think she is not there.

KING.
> 'Tis then no time to dally. You o'the guard,
> Wait at the back door of the prince's lodging 80
> And see that none pass thence, upon your lives.
> Knock, gentlemen. Knock loud. Louder yet!

---

59. *crossly*] "in a way that crosses [thwarts] ordinary affinities" *(OED,* citing this passage).

II.iv   PHILASTER

>What, has their pleasure taken off their hearing?
>I'll break your meditations. Knock again.
>Not yet? I do not think he sleeps, having his   85
>Larum by him. Once more. Pharamond, prince!

>>*[Enter]* Pharamond *above.*

PHARAMOND.
>What saucy groom knocks at this dead of night?
>Where be our waiters? By my vexed soul,
>He meets his death that meets me for this boldness.

KING.
>Prince, you wrong your thoughts. We are your friends.   90
>Come down.

PHARAMOND.   The king!
KING.   The same, sir. Come down.
>We have cause of present counsel with you.

>>*[Exit]* Pharamond *[and enter] below.*

PHARAMOND.
>If your grace please to use me, I'll attend you
>To your chamber.

KING.
>No, 'tis too late, prince. I'll make bold with yours.   95

PHARAMOND.
>I have some private reasons to myself
>Makes me unmannerly and say you cannot.
>Nay, press not forward, gentlemen. He must come
>Through my life that comes here.

KING.
>Sir, be resolv'd I must and will come. Enter!   100

---

    84. *your meditations*] Turner emends to "their meditations" because two Q1 occurrences of *your* in the previous line have been altered to *their* in Q2 and the annotator (or compositor) may have missed this third occurrence.
    86. *Larum*] alarm, summons to warn or awake.
    88. *waiters*] watchmen.
    89. *that meets me*] who opposes or fights with me.
    92.1.] Turner's stage direction; Q2, "Pharamond *below.*" Pharamond leaves the upper stage and re-enters on the lower stage.

—44—

PHARAMOND.
>I will not be dishonor'd.
>He that enters, enters upon his death.
>Sir, 'tis a sign you make no stranger of me
>To bring these renegados to my chamber
>At these unseason'd hours.

KING.   Why do you
>Chafe yourself so? You are not wrong'd nor shall be.
>Only I'll search your lodging for some cause
>To ourself known. Enter, I say.

PHARAMOND.   I say no.

[Enter] Megra above.

MEGRA.
>Let 'em enter, prince, let 'em enter.
>I am up and ready. I know their business.
>'Tis the poor breaking of a lady's honor
>They hunt so hotly after. Let 'em enjoy it.
>You have your business, gentlemen; I lay here.
>Oh my lord the king, this is not noble in you
>To make public the weakness of a woman.

KING.
>Come down.

MEGRA.
>I dare, my lord. Your whootings and your clamors,
>Your private whispers and your broad fleerings,
>Can no more vex my soul than this base carriage.
>But I have vengeance yet in store for some
>Shall, in the most contempt you can have of me,
>Be joy and nourishment.

KING.   Will you come down?

---

104. *renegados*] renegades; "used vaguely as a term of abuse" *(OED,* citing this passage).
117. *whootings*] an obsolete variant of hoot or hootings *(OED).*
118. *fleerings*] sneers, gibes (Onions).
119. *carriage*] "action of conducting, carrying out; execution; conduct, management, administration" *(OED).*

II.iv   PHILASTER

MEGRA.
> Yes, to laugh at your worst, but I shall wring you
> If my skill fail me not.   [*Exit*] Megra *above.*

KING.
> Sir, I must dearly chide you for this looseness.   125
> You have wrong'd a worthy lady. But no more;
> Conduct him to my lodging and to bed.
>   *Exeunt* Pharamond *and attendants.*

CLEREMONT.
> Get him another wench and you bring him to bed indeed.

DION.
> 'Tis strange a man cannot ride a stage
> Or two to breathe himself without a warrant.   130
> If this gear hold, that lodgings be search'd thus,
> Pray God we may lie with our own wives in safety,
> That they be not by some trick of state mistaken!

Enter [guards] with Megra.

KING.
> Now, lady of honor, where's your honor now?
> No man can fit your palate but the prince.   135
> Thou most ill-shrouded rottenness, thou piece
> Made by a painter and a 'pothecary,
> Thou troubled sea of lust, thou wilderness
> Inhabited by wild thoughts, thou swollen cloud
> Of infection, thou ripe mine of all diseases,   140
> Thou all sin, all hell, and last, all devils! Tell me,
> Had you none to pull on with your courtesies

---

    123. *wring*] cause distress or anguish to someone *(OED)*.
    129. *stage*] the Q1 reading, conjecturally arrived at by Theobald and adopted by later editors; Q2–F read *stag. Stage* is used in the sense of a distance between two stations or rest-places on a trip. "There is an allusion to the necessity, at the period, of obtaining a warrant for the hire of post-horses" (Boas).
    131. *gear*] doings, goings-on; also business, affair, matter *(OED)*.
    133.1.] Dyce emends to *"Enter* Megra *below."* Q1 gives the direction *"they come down to the King."*
    137. *'pothecary*] apothecary, druggist.
    142. *pull on*] entice.

PHILASTER
II.iv

But he that must be mine, and wrong my daughter?
By all the gods, all these and all the pages
And all the court shall hoot thee through the court, 145
Fling rotten oranges, make ribald rhymes,
And sear thy name with candles upon walls.
Do you laugh, Lady Venus?

MEGRA.

Faith, sir, you must pardon me.
I cannot choose but laugh to see you merry. 150
If you do this, oh king, nay if you dare do it,
By all those gods you swore by and as many
More of mine own, I will have fellows, and such
Fellows in it, as shall make noble mirth.
The princess, your dear daughter, shall stand by me 155
On walls and sung in ballads, anything.
Urge me no more. I know her and her haunts,
Her lays, leaps, and outlays, and will discover all;
Nay, will dishonor her. I know the boy
She keeps, a handsome boy about eighteen, 160
Know what she does with him, where and when.
Come, sir, you put me to a woman's madness,
The glory of a fury, and if I do not
Do it to the height—

KING.   What boy is this she raves at?

MEGRA.

Alas, good-minded prince, you know not these things. 165
I am loath to reveal 'em. Keep this fault
As you would keep your health from the hot air
Of the corrupted people, or by heaven
I will not fall alone. What I have known
Shall be as public as a print. All tongues 170
Shall speak it as they do the language they
Are born in, as free and commonly. I'll set it
Like a prodigious star for all to gaze at,

---

153. *fellows*] companions.
158. *lays . . . outlays*] OED cites this passage in listing obsolete or dialectal uses of *outlay*, as in "an out-lying or out-of-the-way lair." *Lays* and *leaps* refer to the alleged sportive activities.
173. *prodigious*] portentous (Dyce).

—47—

II.iv   PHILASTER

And so high and glowing that other kingdoms far and foreign
Shall read it there, nay travel with it, till they find   175
No tongue to make it more, nor no more people.
And then behold the fall of your fair princess.

KING.
Has she a boy?

CLEREMONT.
So please your grace, I have seen a boy wait
On her, a fair boy.

KING.   Go, get you to your quarter.   180
For this time I'll study to forget you.

MEGRA.
Do you study to forget me, and I'll study
To forget you.   *Exeunt* King, Megra, *guard.*

CLEREMONT.
Why, here's a male spirit fit for Hercules. If ever there
be Nine Worthies of women, this wench shall ride astride   185
and be their captain.

DION.
Sure she has a garrison of devils in her tongue, she
utter'd such balls of wildfire. She has so nettled the king
that all the doctors in the country will scarce cure him.
That boy was a strange-found-out antidote to cure her   190
infections. That boy, that princess' boy; that brave,
chaste, virtuous lady's boy; and a fair boy, a well-spoken
boy! All these consider'd can make nothing else—but
there I leave you, gentlemen.

THRASILINE.
Nay, we'll go wander with you.   *Exeunt.* 195

[III.i]   *Enter* Cleremont, Dion, Thrasiline.

CLEREMONT.
Nay, doubtless 'tis true.

---

185. *Nine Worthies*] chief heroes of history and legend; an early listing appears in William Caxton's Preface to Malory's *Morte D'Arthur* (1485). Included are three pagans (Hector, Alexander, Julius Caesar), three Jews (Joshua, David, Judas Maccabeus), and three Christians (Charlemagne, Godfrey of Bouillon, Arthur).

PHILASTER III.i

DION. Ay, and 'tis the gods
That rais'd this punishment to scourge the king
With his own issue. Is it not a shame
For us that should write noble in the land,
For us that should be free men, to behold 5
A man that is the bravery of his age,
Philaster, press'd down from his royal right
By this regardless king? And only look
And see the scepter ready to be cast
Into the hands of that lascivious lady 10
That lives in lust with a smooth boy, now to be
Married to yon strange prince who, but that people
Please to let him be a prince, is born a slave
In that which should be his most noble part,
His mind.
THRASILINE. That man that would not stir with you 15
To aid Philaster, let the gods forget
That such a creature walks upon the earth!
CLEREMONT.
Philaster is too backward in't himself.
The gentry do await it, and the people
Against their nature are all bent for him, 20
And like a field of standing corn that's mov'd
With a stiff gale, their heads bow all one way.
DION.
The only cause that draws Philaster back
From this attempt is the fair princess' love
Which he admires and we can now confute. 25
THRASILINE.
Perhaps he'll not believe it.
DION.
Why, gentlemen, 'tis without question so.
CLEREMONT.
Ay, 'tis past speech, she lives dishonestly.
But how shall we, if he be curious, work

---

4. *write*] set oneself down as, call oneself, lay claim to (Onions).
29. *curious*] particular, cautious, as about details or a manner of action *(OED)*; also, scrupulous (Weber).

—49—

III.i　　　　　　　　　PHILASTER

　　　Upon his faith?　　　　　　　　　　　　　　　30
THRASILINE.
　　　We all are satisfied within ourselves.
DION.
　　　Since it is true and tends to his own good,
　　　I'll make this new report to be my knowledge.
　　　I'll say I know it; nay, I'll swear I saw it.
CLEREMONT.
　　　It will be best.　　　　　　　　　　　　　　35
THRASILINE.
　　　'Twill move him.

　　　　　　　　　Enter Philaster.

DION.
　　　Here he comes. Good morrow to your honor.
　　　We have spent some time in seeking you.
PHILASTER.
　　　My worthy friends,
　　　You that can keep your memories to know　　40
　　　Your friend in miseries and cannot frown
　　　On men disgrac'd for virtue, a good day
　　　Attend you all! What service may I do
　　　Worthy your acceptation?
DION.　　　　　　　　　My good lord,
　　　We come to urge that virtue which we know　45
　　　Lives in your breast, forth; rise and make a head!
　　　The nobles and the people are all dull'd
　　　With this usurping king, and not a man
　　　That ever heard the word or known such a thing
　　　As virtue but will second your attempts.　　　50
PHILASTER.
　　　How honorable is this love in you
　　　To me that have deserv'd none! Know, my friends,
　　　You that were born to shame your poor Philaster
　　　With too much courtesy, I could afford
　　　To melt myself to thanks. But my designs　　55
　　　Are not yet ripe. Suffice it that ere long

---

46. *make a head*] "raise a body of troops" *(OED)*.

PHILASTER   III.i

    I shall employ your loves, but yet the time
    Is short of what I would.
DION.
    The time is fuller, sir, than you expect.
    That which hereafter will not perhaps be reach'd   60
    By violence, may now be caught. As for the king,
    You know the people have long hated him.
    But now the princess, whom they lov'd—
PHILASTER.
    Why, what of her?
DION.   Is loath'd as much as he.
PHILASTER.
    By what strange means?
DION.   She's known a whore.   65
PHILASTER.
    Thou liest!
DION.   My lord—
PHILASTER.   Thou liest, *Offers to draw and is held.*
    And thou shalt feel it. I had thought thy mind
    Had been of honor. Thus to rob a lady
    Of her good name is an infectious sin
    Not to be pardon'd. Be it false as hell   70
    'Twill never be redeem'd if it be sown
    Amongst the people, fruitful to increase
    All evil they shall hear. Let me alone
    That I may cut off falsehood whilst it springs.
    Set hills on hills betwixt me and the man   75
    That utters this, and I will scale them all
    And from the utmost top fall on his neck
    Like thunder from a cloud!
DION.   This is most strange.
    Sure he does love her.
PHILASTER.   I do love fair truth;
    She is my mistress, and who injures her   80
    Draws vengeance from me. Sirs, let go my arms.
THRASILINE.
    Nay, good my lord, be patient.
CLEREMONT.
    Sir, remember this is your honor'd friend

III.i   PHILASTER

        That comes to do his service and will show you
        Why he utter'd this.
PHILASTER.   I ask you pardon, sir.   85
        My zeal to truth made me unmannerly.
        Should I have heard dishonor spoke of you
        Behind your back untruly, I had been
        As much distemper'd and enrag'd as now.
DION.
        But this, my lord, is truth.   90
PHILASTER.
        Oh, say not so, good sir; forbear to say so!
        'Tis then truth that womankind is false.
        Urge it no more, it is impossible.
        Why should you think the princess light?
DION.
        Why, she was taken at it.   95
PHILASTER.
        'Tis false, by heaven, 'tis false. It cannot be,
        Can it? Speak, gentlemen, for God's love speak!
        Is't possible? Can women all be damn'd?
DION.
        Why no, my lord.
PHILASTER.   Why then it cannot be.
DION.
        And she was taken with her boy.
PHILASTER.   What boy?   100
DION.
        A page, a boy that serves her.
PHILASTER.
        Oh good gods, a little boy?
DION.
        Ay; know you him, my lord?
PHILASTER.
        Hell and sin know him! Sir, you are deceiv'd.
        I'll reason it a little coldly with you.   105
        If she were lustful, would she take a boy
        That knows not yet desire? She would have one
        Should meet her thoughts and know the sin he acts,
        Which is the great delight of wickedness.

PHILASTER   III.i

    You are abus'd, and so is she and I.   110
DION.
    How you, my lord?
PHILASTER.   Why, all the world's abus'd
    In an unjust report.
DION.   Oh noble sir, your virtues
    Cannot look into the subtle thoughts of woman.
    In short, my lord, I took them; I myself.
PHILASTER.
    Now, all the devils, thou didst! Fly from my rage.   115
    Would thou hadst ta'en devils engend'ring plagues
    When thou didst take them. Hide thee from mine eyes!
    Would thou hadst ta'en thunder on thy breast
    When thou didst take them, or been strucken dumb
    Forever, that this foul deed might have slept   120
    In silence.
THRASILINE [aside]. Have you known him so ill-temper'd?
CLEREMONT.
    Never before.
PHILASTER.   The winds that are let loose
    From the four several corners of the earth
    And spread themselves all over sea and land,
    Kiss not a chaste one. What friend bears a sword   125
    To run me through?
DION.
    Why, my lord, are you so mov'd at this?
PHILASTER.
    When any fall from virtue, I am distracted.
    I have an interest in't.
DION.
    But, good my lord, recall yourself   130
    And think what's best to be done.
PHILASTER.
    I thank you; I will do it.
    Please you to leave me. I'll consider of it.

---

128. *distracted*] troubled in mind, perplexed, sometimes to the extent of mental derangement *(OED)*.

III.i   PHILASTER

    Tomorrow I will find your lodging forth
    And give you answer.
DION.   All the gods direct you   135
    The readiest way.
THRASILINE [*aside*].   He was extreme impatient.
CLEREMONT [*aside*].
    It was his virtue and his noble mind.
                     Exeunt Dion, Cleremont, Thrasiline.
PHILASTER.
    I had forgot to ask him where he took them.
    I'll follow him. Oh, that I had a sea
    Within my breast to quench the fire I feel!   140
    More circumstances will but fan this fire.
    It more afflicts me now to know by whom
    This deed is done than simply that 'tis done,
    And he that tells me this is honorable,
    As far from lies as she is far from truth.   145
    Oh, that like beasts we could not grieve ourselves
    With that we see not! Bulls and rams will fight
    To keep their females, standing in their sight;
    But take 'em from them and you take at once
    Their spleens away, and they will fall again   150
    Unto their pastures, growing fresh and fat,
    And taste the waters of the springs as sweet
    As 'twas before, finding no start in sleep.
    But miserable man—

              Enter Bellario.

                 See, see, you gods,
    He walks still, and the face you let him wear   155
    When he was innocent is still the same,
    Not blasted. Is this justice? Do you mean
    To entrap mortality, that you allow
    Treason so smooth a brow? I cannot now
    Think he is guilty.

---

    150. *spleens*] "high spirit, courage, resolute mind" *(OED)*. The spleen was once believed to be the seat of such emotions as moroseness, anger, and at times mirth.

BELLARIO. Health to you, my lord. 160
    The princess doth commend her love, her life,
    And this unto you.   [*Gives* Philaster *a letter.*]
PHILASTER.   Oh, Bellario,
    Now I perceive she loves me. She does show it
    In loving thee, my boy. She has made thee brave.
BELLARIO.
    My lord, she has attir'd me past my wish, 165
    Past my desert; more fit for her attendant,
    Though far unfit for me who do attend.
PHILASTER.
    Thou art grown courtly, boy. Oh, let all women
    That love black deeds learn to dissemble here,
    Here, by this paper! She does write to me 170
    As if her heart were mines of adamant
    To all the world besides, but unto me
    A maiden snow that melted with my looks.
    Tell me, my boy, how doth the princess use thee?
    For I shall guess her love to me by that. 175
BELLARIO.
    Scarce like her servant, but as if I were
    Something allied to her or had preserv'd
    Her life three times by my fidelity;
    As mothers fond do use their only sons;
    As I'd use one that's left unto my trust 180
    For whom my life should pay if he met harm.
    So she does use me.
PHILASTER.   Why, this is wondrous well.
    But what kind language does she feed thee with?
BELLARIO.
    Why, she does tell me she will trust my youth
    With all her loving secrets and does call me 185
    Her pretty servant; bids me weep no more

---

164. *brave*] richly dressed, as at II.iv.26.
171. *adamant*] "name of an alleged rock or mineral, as to which vague, contradictory, and fabulous notions long prevailed" *(OED)*. The usual property ascribed to it is a diamond-like hardness, as in this passage; at times it is considered magnetic like the loadstone.

III.i   PHILASTER

        For leaving you, she'll see my services
        Regarded; and such words of that soft strain
        That I am nearer weeping when she ends
        Than ere she spake.

PHILASTER.   This is much better still.   190

BELLARIO.
        Are you not ill, my lord?

PHILASTER.   Ill? No, Bellario.

BELLARIO.
        Methinks your words
        Fall not from off your tongue so evenly,
        Nor is there in your looks that quietness
        That I was wont to see.

PHILASTER.   Thou art deceiv'd, boy.   195
        And she strokes thy head?

BELLARIO.   Yes.

PHILASTER.
        And she does clap thy cheeks?

BELLARIO.   She does, my lord.

PHILASTER.
        And she does kiss thee, boy? Ha?

BELLARIO.   How, my lord?

PHILASTER.
        She kisses thee?

BELLARIO.   Never, my lord, by heaven.

PHILASTER.
        That's strange. I know she does.

BELLARIO.   No, by my life.   200

PHILASTER.
        Why, then, she does not love me. Come, she does.
        I bade her do it. I charg'd her, by all charms
        Of love between us, by the hope of peace
        We should enjoy, to yield thee all delights
        Naked as to her bed. I took her oath   205
        Thou shouldst enjoy her. Tell me, gentle boy,
        Is she not parallel-less? Is not her breath

---

    207. *parallel-less*] Q1 reads *paradise*, Q2-4 *parrallesse*, Q5-8 and F *parallel-lesse*. Turner comments on the Q2 reading: "Although this

—56—

Sweet as Arabian winds when fruits are ripe?
Are not her breasts two liquid ivory balls?
Is she not all a lasting mine of joy? 210
BELLARIO.
Ay, now I see why my disturbed thoughts
Were so perplex'd. When first I went to her,
My heart held augury. You are abus'd;
Some villain has abus'd you. I do see
Whereto you tend. Fall rocks upon his head 215
That put this to you. 'Tis some subtle train
To bring that noble frame of yours to nought.
PHILASTER.
Thou think'st I will be angry with thee. Come,
Thou shalt know all my drift. I hate her more
Than I love happiness and plac'd thee there 220
To pry with narrow eyes into her deeds.
Hast thou discover'd? Is she fallen to lust
As I would wish her? Speak some comfort to me.
BELLARIO.
My lord, you did mistake the boy you sent.
Had she the lust of sparrows or of goats, 225
Had she a sin that way, hid from the world,
Beyond the name of lust, I would not aid
Her base desires. But what I came to know
As servant to her, I would not reveal
To make my life last ages.
PHILASTER.   Oh, my heart! 230
This is a salve worse than the main disease.
Tell me thy thoughts, for I will know the least
That dwells within thee or will rip thy heart
To know it. I will see thy thoughts as plain
As I do now thy face.
BELLARIO.   Why, so you do. 235
She is, for aught I know, by all the gods

---

unusual word may be a mistake for *parallel-lesse*, there is a good chance that it is an eccentric spelling of 'pareil-less' [without equal, as in "nonpareil"]. 'Pareil,' for which the *OED* records such spellings as 'parelle' and 'parail,' could be used as an adjective."

221. *narrow*] "strict, close, precise, careful" *(OED)*.

III.i   PHILASTER

    As chaste as ice. But were she foul as hell
    And I did know it thus, the breath of kings,
    The points of swords, tortures, nor bulls of brass
    Should draw it from me.   240
PHILASTER.
    Then 'tis no time to dally with thee.
    I will take thy life, for I do hate thee.
    I could curse thee now.
BELLARIO.
    If you do hate, you could not curse me worse.
    The gods have not a punishment in store   245
    Greater for me than is your hate.
PHILASTER.
    Fie, fie, so young and so dissembling!
    Tell me when and where thou didst enjoy her,
    Or let plagues fall on me if I destroy thee not.
BELLARIO.
    By heaven, I never did, and when I lie   250
    To save my life, may I live long and loath'd.   [*Kneels*.]
    Hew me asunder, and whilst I can think
    I'll love those pieces you have cut away
    Better than those that grow, and kiss those limbs
    Because you made 'em so.
PHILASTER.   Fear'st thou not death?   255
    Can boys contemn that?
BELLARIO.   Oh, what boy is he
    Can be content to live to be a man
    That sees the best of men thus passionate,
    Thus without reason?
PHILASTER.
    Oh, but thou dost not know what 'tis to die.   260
BELLARIO.
    Yes, I do know, my lord.
    'Tis less than to be born; a lasting sleep,
    A quiet resting from all jealousy,

---

  239. *bulls of brass*] an allusion to the story of the tyrant Phalaris and his instrument of torture which caused death by roasting.
  256. *contemn*] despise, as at I.ii.92.

                    A thing we all pursue. I know besides
                    It is but giving over of a game   265
                    That must be lost.
PHILASTER.   But there are pains, false boy,
                    For perjur'd souls. Think but on those, and then
                    Thy heart will melt and thou wilt utter all.
BELLARIO.
                    May they fall all upon me whilst I live
                    If I be perjur'd or have ever thought   270
                    Of that you charge me with. If I be false,
                    Send me to suffer in those punishments
                    You speak of. Kill me.
PHILASTER.   Oh, what should I do?
                    Why, who can but believe him? He does swear
                    So earnestly that if it were not true   275
                    The gods would not endure him. Rise, Bellario.
                    Thy protestations are so deep and thou
                    Dost look so truly when thou utter'st them
                    That, though I know 'em false as were my hopes,
                    I cannot urge thee further. But thou wert   280
                    To blame to injure me, for I must love
                    Thy honest looks and take no revenge upon
                    Thy tender youth. A love from me to thee
                    Is firm whate'er thou doest. It troubles me
                    That I have call'd the blood out of thy cheeks   285
                    That did so well become thee. But, good boy,
                    Let me not see thee more. Something is done
                    That will distract me, that will make me mad,
                    If I behold thee. If thou tender'st me,
                    Let me not see thee.
BELLARIO.   I will fly as far   290
                    As there is morning ere I give distaste
                    To that most honor'd mind. But through these tears
                    Shed at my hopeless parting, I can see
                    A world of treason practic'd upon you
                    And her and me. Farewell forever more.   295
                    If you shall hear that sorrow struck me dead

---

289. *tender'st*] have a tender regard for, be concerned for (Onions).

III.i   PHILASTER

    And after find me loyal, let there be
    A tear shed from you in my memory
    And I shall rest at peace.   *Exit* Bellario.

PHILASTER.   Blessing be with thee
    Whatever thou deservest. Oh, where shall I   300
    Go bathe this body? Nature too unkind
    That made no medicine for a troubled mind. *Exit* Philaster.

[III.ii]   *Enter* Arethusa.

ARETHUSA.
    I marvel my boy comes not back again.
    But that I know my love will question him
    Over and over—how I slept, wak'd, talk'd,
    How I remember'd him when his dear name
    Was last spoke, and how when I sigh'd, wept, sung,   5
    And ten thousand such—I should be angry
    At his stay.

                  Enter King.

KING.
    What, at your meditations? Who attends you?

ARETHUSA.
    None but my single self. I need no guard.
    I do no wrong, nor fear none.   10

KING.
    Tell me, have you not a boy?

ARETHUSA.
    Yes, sir.

KING.
    What kind of boy?

ARETHUSA.
    A page, a waiting-boy.

KING.
    A handsome boy?   15

ARETHUSA.
    I think he be not ugly.
    Well qualified and dutiful I know him.
    I took him not for beauty.

KING.
>   He speaks and sings and plays?
ARETHUSA.
>   Yes, sir. 20
KING.
>   About eighteen?
ARETHUSA.
>   I never ask'd his age.
KING.
>   Is he full of service?
ARETHUSA.
>   By your pardon, why do you ask?
KING.
>   Put him away. 25
ARETHUSA.
>   Sir!
KING.
>   Put him away, I say. H'as done you that good service
>   Shames me to speak of.
ARETHUSA.
>   Good sir, let me understand you.
KING.
>   If you fear me, 30
>   Show it in duty. Put away that boy.
ARETHUSA.
>   Let me have reason for it, sir, and then
>   Your will is my command.
KING.
>   Do not you blush to ask it? Cast him off
>   Or I shall do the same to you. Y'are one 35
>   Shame with me, and so near unto myself
>   That by my life I dare not tell myself
>   What you, myself, have done.
ARETHUSA.
>   What I have done, my lord?

---

37. *by my life*] Turner follows the Q1 reading *by the gods* here and at V.iii.123 *(by all the gods),* suspecting some euphemism of oaths in Q2.

III.ii   PHILASTER

KING.
'Tis a new language that all love to learn.   40
The common people speak it well already:
They need no grammar. Understand me well,
There be foul whispers stirring. Cast him off
And suddenly. Do it! Farewell.   *Exit* King.

ARETHUSA.
Where may a maiden live securely free,   45
Keeping her honor fair? Not with the living.
They feed upon opinions, errors, dreams,
And make 'em truths. They draw a nourishment
Out of defamings, grow upon disgraces;
And when they see a virtue fortified   50
Strongly above the batt'ry of their tongues,
Oh how they cast to sink it; and defeated,
Soul sick with poison, strike the monuments
Where noble names lie sleeping till they sweat
And the cold marble melt.   55

Enter Philaster.

PHILASTER.
Peace to your fairest thoughts, dearest mistress.

ARETHUSA.
Oh, my dearest servant, I have a war within me.

PHILASTER.
He must be more than man that makes these crystals
Run into rivers. Sweetest fair, the cause?
And as I am your slave, tied to your goodness,   60
Your creature made again from what I was
And newly spirited, I'll right your honor.

ARETHUSA.
Oh, my best love, that boy!

PHILASTER.
What boy?

ARETHUSA.
The pretty boy you gave me—   65

PHILASTER.
What of him?

ARETHUSA.
    Must be no more mine.
PHILASTER.
    Why?
ARETHUSA.
    They are jealous of him.
PHILASTER.
    Jealous? Who?   70
ARETHUSA.
    The king.
PHILASTER [*aside*].
    Oh my misfortune!
    Then 'tis no idle jealousy. —Let him go.
ARETHUSA.
    Oh cruel, are you hard-hearted too?
    Who shall now tell you how much I lov'd you?   75
    Who shall swear it to you and weep the tears I send?
    Who shall now bring you letters, rings, bracelets?
    Lose his health in service? Wake tedious nights
    In stories of your praise? Who shall sing
    Your crying elegies, and strike a sad soul   80
    Into senseless pictures and make them mourn?
    Who shall take up his lute and touch it till
    He crown a silent sleep upon my eyelids,
    Making me dream and cry oh my dear,
    Dear Philaster?
PHILASTER [*aside*]. Oh my heart!   85
    Would he had broken thee that made thee know
    This lady was not loyal. —Mistress, forget
    The boy. I'll get thee a far better.
ARETHUSA.
    Oh never, never such a boy again
    As my Bellario.
PHILASTER.   'Tis but your fond affection.   90
ARETHUSA.
    With thee, my boy, farewell forever
    All secrecy in servants. Farewell faith

---

75. *lov'd you*] Turner emends to "love you."

III.ii   PHILASTER

        And all desire to do well for itself.
        Let all that shall succeed thee, for thy wrongs
        Sell and betray chaste love.   95
PHILASTER.
        And all this passion for a boy?
ARETHUSA.
        He was your boy and you put him to me,
        And the loss of such must have a mourning for.
PHILASTER.
        Oh thou forgetful woman!
ARETHUSA.   How, my lord?
PHILASTER.
        False Arethusa!   100
        Hast thou a medicine to restore my wits
        When I have lost 'em? If not, leave to talk
        And do thus.
ARETHUSA.   Do what, sir? Would you sleep?
PHILASTER.
        Forever, Arethusa. Oh you gods,
        Give me a worthy patience. Have I stood   105
        Naked, alone, the shock of many fortunes?
        Have I seen mischiefs numberless and mighty
        Grow like a sea upon me? Have I taken
        Danger as stern as death into my bosom
        And laugh'd upon it, made it but a mirth,   110
        And flung it by? Do I live now like him,
        Under this tyrant king, that languishing
        Hears his sad bell and sees his mourners? Do I
        Bear all this bravely and must sink at length
        Under a woman's falsehood? Oh that boy,   115
        That cursed boy! None but a villain boy
        To ease your lust?
ARETHUSA.   Nay, then, I am betray'd.
        I feel the plot cast for my overthrow.
        Oh I am wretched!
PHILASTER.
        Now you may take that little right I have   120

---

113. *Hears . . . bell*] imagines his own funeral.

PHILASTER   III.ii

To this poor kingdom. Give it to your joy,
For I have no joy in it. Some far place
Where never womankind durst set her foot
Forbursting with her poisons, must I seek
And live to curse you.   125
There dig a cave and preach to birds and beasts
What woman is and help to save them from you.
How heaven is in your eyes but in your hearts
More hell than hell has. How your tongues, like scorpions,
Both heal and poison. How your thoughts are woven   130
With thousand changes in one subtle web
And worn so by you. How that foolish man
That reads the story of a woman's face
And dies believing it is lost forever.
How all the good you have is but a shadow,   135
I'th' morning with you and at night behind you,
Past and forgotten. How your vows are frosts,
Fast for a night and with the next sun gone.
How you are, being taken all together,
A mere confusion and so dead a chaos   140
That love cannot distinguish. These sad texts
Till my last hour I am bound to utter of you.
So farewell all my woe, all my delight!   *Exit* Philaster.
ARETHUSA.
Be merciful, ye gods, and strike me dead.
What way have I deserv'd this? Make my breast   145
Transparent as pure crystal that the world,
Jealous of me, may see the foulest thought
My heart holds. Where shall a woman turn her eyes
To find out constancy?

---

124. *Forbursting*] may have the obsolete sense of bursting completely, "for" being the intensifying prefix (Turner notes this possible meaning); here used to describe womankind's foot. Mason, quoted by Weber, suggests the meaning is "for fear of bursting . . . . It was vulgarly supposed that there were places where no venomous creatures could live."

129. *like scorpions*] "The flesh of the scorpion was supposed to be a cure for its own sting" *(OED)*.

138. *Fast*] secure.

—65—

III.ii   PHILASTER

Enter Bellario.

                              Save me, how black
And guiltily methinks that boy looks now!   150
Oh thou dissembler, that before thou spak'st
Wert in thy cradle false, sent to make lies
And betray innocents! Thy lord and thou
May glory in the ashes of a maid
Fool'd by her passion, but the conquest is   155
Nothing so great as wicked. Fly away!
Let my command force thee to that which shame
Would do without it. If thou understood'st
The loathed office thou hast undergone,
Why, thou wouldst hide thee under heaps of hills   160
Lest men should dig and find thee.
BELLARIO.   Oh what god,
Angry with men, hath sent this strange disease
Into the noblest minds? Madam, this grief
You add unto me is no more than drops
To seas, for which they are not seen to swell.   165
My lord hath struck his anger through my heart
And let out all the hope of future joys.
You need not bid me fly. I came to part,
To take my latest leave. Farewell forever.
I durst not run away in honesty   170
From such a lady, like a boy that stole
Or made some grievous fault. The power of gods
Assist you in your sufferings! Hasty time
Reveal the truth to your abused lord
And mine, that he may know your worth, whilst I   175
Go seek out some forgotten place to die.   *Exit* Bellario.
ARETHUSA.
Peace guide thee. Th'ast overthrown me once.

---

  169. *latest*] last.
  177–181. *Peace . . . streets*] John Masefield has called these five lines "the loveliest thing in the play" (*Atlantic*, CXCIX, 73). Theobald comments: "The Image seems here plainly to be shadow'd from the Picture of Hecuba, drawn by Shakespeare in his *Hamlet*, as running about the Streets of *Troy* in the midst of the Flames." Cf. "the mobled Queen" passage in *Hamlet*, II.ii.524–541.

Yet if I had another Troy to lose,
Thou or another villain with thy looks
Might talk me out of it and send me naked, 180
My hair dishevel'd, through the fiery streets.

Enter a Lady.

LADY.
Madam, the king would hunt and calls for you
With earnestness.
ARETHUSA.   I am in tune to hunt.
Diana, if thou canst rage with a maid
As with a man, let me discover thee 185
Bathing and turn me to a fearful hind,
That I may die pursu'd by cruel hounds
And have my story written in my wounds.

Exeunt.

[IV.i] *Enter* King, *Pharamond*, Arethusa, *Galatea, Megra*, Dion, Cleremont, Thrasiline, *and attendants.*

KING.
What, are the hounds before and all the woodmen,
Our horses ready and our bows bent?
DION.
All, sir.
KING [*to* Pharamond].
Y'are cloudy, sir. Come, we have forgotten
Your venial trespass. Let not that sit heavy 5
Upon your spirit. Here's none dare utter it.

---

184. *Diana*] also called Artemis, goddess of the hunt and protectress of the innocent. The mythological Arethusa was in her service when turned into a fountain to escape Alpheus. The man referred to in l. 185 is Actaeon, who was turned into a stag and killed by his own hounds as punishment for seeing Diana bathing naked in a stream.
[IV.i]
1. *before*] ahead.
1. *woodmen*] game hunters in a wood or forest *(OED)*.
4. *cloudy*] gloomy, downcast.
5. *venial*] excusable.

IV.i PHILASTER

DION [*aside*].
  He looks like an old surfeited stallion after his leaping, dull as a dormouse. See how he sinks. The wench has shot him between wind and water, and I hope sprung a leak. 10

THRASILINE [*aside*].
  He needs no teaching, he strikes sure enough. His greatest fault is he hunts too much in the purlieus. Would he would leave off poaching.

DION [*aside*].
  And for his horn, h'as left it at the lodge where he lay late. Oh, he's a precious lime-hound. Turn him loose 15
upon the pursue of a lady and if he lose her, hang him up i'th' slip. When my fox-bitch Beauty grows proud, I'll borrow him.

KING.
  Is your boy turn'd away?

ARETHUSA.
  You did command, sir, and I obey'd you. 20

KING.
  'Tis well done. Hark ye further. [*They talk apart.*]

CLEREMONT.
  Is't possible this fellow should repent? Methinks that were not noble in him. And yet he looks like a mortified member, as if he had a sick man's salve in's mouth. If a

---

12. *purlieus*] originally disafforested lands, withdrawn as hunting preserves and often remitted to the former owners; also, land on the border of a forest. Here, to pursue illicit love (*OED*, citing this passage).

15. *lime-hound*] lyam-hound or bloodhound (lyam=leash); *OED* cites this passage as an example of the figurative application to persons who pursue.

16. *pursue*] the reading of Q1-3, followed by Turner who notes the *OED* definition of *pursue*: "the trail of blood left by a wounded animal." Other editors have adopted the Q4 reading, *pursuit*.

17. *slip*] "noose in which greyhounds are held" (Onions).

17. *grows proud*] is in heat.

23. *mortified*] as if dead; rendered insensible (*OED*).

24. *sick man's salve*] title of a work (1561) by Thomas Becon on Christian attitudes toward sickness and death; frequently alluded to in pamphlets and plays with ridicule (Dyce).

worse man had done this fault now, some physical justice 25
or other would presently, without the help of an almanac, have open'd the obstructions of his liver and let him
blood with a dog whip.

DION.

See, see, how modestly yon lady looks, as if she came
from churching with her neighbors. Why, what a devil 30
can a man see in her face but that she's honest?

THRASILINE.

Faith, no great matter to speak of; a foolish twinkling
with the eye that spoils her coat, but he must be a
cunning herald that finds it.

DION.

See how they muster one another! Oh, there's a rank 35
regiment where the devil carries the colors and his dam
drum-major. Now the world and the flesh come behind
with the carriage.

CLEREMONT.

Sure this lady has a good turn done her against her will.
Before, she was common talk; now none dare say can- 40
tharides can stir her. Her face looks like a warrant,
willing and commanding all tongues, as they will answer
it, to be tied up and bolted when this lady means to let
herself loose. As I live, she has got her a goodly protec-
tion, and a gracious, and may use her body discreetly 45
for her health's sake once a week, excepting Lent and

---

25. *physical justice*] someone acting as a physician.

26–27. *almanac*] "Old almanacks contained directions as to the suit-able times for blood-letting" (Daniel).

33. *spoils her coat*] "The allusion is to mullets, or stars, introduced into coats of arms, to distinguish the younger branches of a family, which of course denote inferiority" (Mason, quoted by Dyce).

35. *muster*] show up, display, exhibit *(OED)*.

36. *dam*] female parent; "the devil and his dam" had become a proverbial phrase, as had "the world, the flesh, and the devil" alluded to in the next line of this passage.

38. *carriage*] baggage or luggage *(OED)*.

40–41. *cantharides*] a preparation of dried beetles, formerly consid-ered an aphrodisiac *(OED,* citing this passage).

IV.i   PHILASTER

Dog-days. Oh, if they were to be got for money, what
a large sum would come out of the city for these licenses!
KING.
To horse, to horse! We lose the morning, gentlemen. *Exeunt.*

[IV.ii]   *Enter two* Woodmen.

1 WOODMAN.
What, have you lodg'd the deer?
2 WOODMAN.
Yes, they are ready for the bow.
1 WOODMAN.
Who shoots?
2 WOODMAN.
The princess.
1 WOODMAN.
No, she'll hunt.   5
2 WOODMAN.
She'll take a stand, I say.
1 WOODMAN.
Who else?
2 WOODMAN.
Why, the young stranger prince.
1 WOODMAN.
He shall shoot in a stone bow for me. I never lov'd his
beyond-sea-ship since he forsook the say for paying ten   10

---

47. *Dog-days*] "the days about the time of the heliacal rising of the
Dog-star [Sirius], noted from ancient times as the hottest and most
unwholesome period of the year"; dated variously, customarily in
July and August *(OED)*.
48. *licenses*] "It was formerly a branch of revenue to grant licenses
for stews [brothels]" (Weber).
[IV.ii]
1. *lodg'd*] discovered the lodge (shooting position) of *(OED)*.
6. *stand*] a hunting station; "a standing in ambush or in cover"
(OED).
9. *stone bow*] "a cross-bow, which shoots stones" (Dyce).
10. *forsook the say*] "When a Deer is hunted down, and to be cut
up, it is a Ceremony for the Keeper to offer his Knife to a man of
the first Distinction in the Field, that he may rip up the Belly, and
take an Assay [trial] of the Plight and Fatness of the Game. But

PHILASTER IV.ii

shillings. He was there at the fall of a deer and would
needs, out of his mightiness, give ten groats for the
dowcets. Marry, the stewart would have the velvet head
into the bargain, to turf his hat withal. I think he should
love venery; he is an old Sir Tristram. For if you be   15
remember'd, he forsook the stag once to strike a rascal
milking in a meadow, and her he kill'd in the eye. Who
shoots else?

2 WOODMAN.
The lady Galatea.

1 WOODMAN.
That's a good wench, an she would not chide us for   20
tumbling of her women in the brakes. She's liberal, and
by the gods they say she's honest, and whether that be a
fault I have nothing to do. There's all?

2 WOODMAN.
No, one more, Megra.

---

this, as the Woodman says, *Pharamond* declined, to save the customary Fee of Ten Shillings" (Theobald).

12. *groats*] silver coins, worth fourpence (at times, more); coined in 1351-2 and no longer issued for circulation after 1662 *(OED)*.

13. *dowcets*] testes; the tender parts of a kill were customarily presented to the ranking nobleman (Dyce).

13. *velvet head*] horns of the hart, so called from the russet hair or velvet found on the horns when first removed (Dyce, from Turbeville's *The Noble Art of Venery*, 1611).

14. *turf his hat*] re-cover a hat with beaver's fur or silk (Dyce).

15. *venery*] hunting.

15. *Sir Tristram*] "an expert huntsman, —that hero of romance being reputed the patron of the chase, and the first who brought hunting to a science" (Dyce).

16-17. *rascal . . . meadow*] *Milking* is the reading found in all early editions, but most modern editors have accepted Theobald's emendation *mitching* (miching), meaning "creeping, solitary, and withdrawn from the Herd"; "A Rascal is a lean Deer, or Doe" (Theobald). Turner argues for the old reading, followed in the present edition: "*Milking* may be understood either as 'giving suck to' (*cf.* OED, V.I.3) or as 'drawing milk from,' in this case, from a cow, the usual inhabitant of a *meadow*. The Woodman means, then, that Pharamond gave over pursuit of the stag to hunt either an undergrown doe suckling her young in a meadow or, much more likely, a lean, inferior doe sucking milk from a cow in a meadow."

20. *an*] if.

IV.ii   PHILASTER

1 WOODMAN.
   That's a firker, i'faith, boy. There's a wench will ride   25
   her haunches as hard after a kennel of hounds as a
   hunting saddle, and when she comes home get 'em clapt
   and all is well again. I have known her lose herself
   three times in one afternoon, if the woods have been
   answerable, and it has been work enough for one man   30
   to find her, and he has sweat for it. She rides well and
   she pays well. Hark, let's go.   *Exeunt.*

[IV.iii]   *Enter* Philaster.

PHILASTER.
   Oh, that I had been nourish'd in these woods
   With milk of goats and acorns and not known
   The right of crowns nor the dissembling trains
   Of women's looks, but digg'd myself a cave
   Where I, my fire, my cattle, and my bed   5
   Might have been shut together in one shed;
   And then had taken me some mountain girl
   Beaten with winds, chaste as the harden'd rocks
   Whereon she dwells, that might have strew'd my bed
   With leaves and reeds and with the skins of beasts,   10
   Our neighbors, and have borne at her big breasts
   My large coarse issue. This had been a life
   Free from vexation.

              Enter Bellario.

BELLARIO.   Oh, wicked men!
   An innocent may walk safe among beasts;
   Nothing assaults me here. See, my grieved lord   15
   Sits as his soul were searching out a way
   To leave his body. Pardon me that must

---

   25. *firker*] a lively, brisk, "jiggish" person; from "firk" meaning to move about briskly, to dance *(OED)*.
   IV.iii] Most editors omit a scene division here, although Daniel mentions the need of one. Turner marks the division.
   1-13. *Oh, that . . . vexation*] "This speech is beautifully imitated from the opening of Juvenal's Sixth Satire" (Dyce).
   16. *as*] as if.

Break thy last commandment, for I must speak.
You that are griev'd can pity. Hear, my lord.
PHILASTER.
Is there a creature yet so miserable
That I can pity?
BELLARIO. Oh, my noble lord,
View my strange fortune and bestow on me
According to your bounty, if my service
Can merit nothing, so much as may serve
To keep that little piece I hold of life
From cold and hunger.
PHILASTER. Is it thou? Be gone.
Go sell those misbeseeming clothes thou wearest
And feed thyself with them.
BELLARIO.
Alas, my lord, I can get nothing for them.
The silly country people think 'tis treason
To touch such gay things.
PHILASTER. Now, by the gods, this is
Unkindly done, to vex me with thy sight.
Thou'rt fallen again to thy dissembling trade.
How shouldst thou think to cozen me again?
Remains there yet a plague untried for me?
Even so thou wept'st and look'st and spok'st when first
I took thee up. Curse on the time! If thy
Commanding tears can work on any other,
Use thy art; I'll not betray it. Which way
Wilt thou take that I may shun thee?
For thine eyes are poison to mine, and I
Am loath to grow in rage. This way or that way?
BELLARIO.
Any will serve, but I will choose to have
That path in chase that leads unto my grave.
Exeunt Philaster, Bellario *severally*.

---

27. *misbeseeming*] unbefitting, inappropriate.
30. *silly*] "unlearned, unsophisticated, simple, rustic, ignorant" *(OED)*.
30. *treason*] breach of faith, trickery.
34. *cozen*] cheat, defraud.
44. *in chase*] in pursuit.

IV.iv   PHILASTER

[IV.iv]   *Enter* Dion *and the* Woodmen.

DION.
  This is the strangest sudden chance! You, woodman.
1 WOODMAN.
  My lord Dion.
DION.
  Saw you a lady come this way on a sable horse studded with stars of white?
2 WOODMAN.
  Was she not young and tall?   5
DION.
  Yes. Rode she to the wood or to the plain?
2 WOODMAN.
  Faith, my lord, we saw none.   *Exeunt* Woodmen.
DION.
  Pox of your questions then!

              Enter Cleremont.

                What, is she found?
CLEREMONT.
  Nor will be, I think.
DION.
  Let him seek his daughter himself. She cannot stray 10
  about a little necessary natural business but the whole
  court must be in arms. When she has done, we shall
  have peace.
CLEREMONT.
  There's already a thousand fatherless tales amongst us.
  Some say her horse ran away with her; some, a wolf 15
  pursu'd her; others, 'twas a plot to kill her and that
  arm'd men were seen in the wood; but questionless she
  rode away willingly.

          Enter King, Thrasiline [*and attendants*].

  IV.iv] This scene division is omitted by most editors except Turner; Daniel, as at IV.iii, mentions the need of a division.
  8. *Pox*] imprecation of irritation or impatience *(OED)*; literally, a disease.

—74—

KING.
>   Where is she?
CLEREMONT.
>   Sir, I cannot tell. 20
KING.
>   How's that? Answer me so again.
CLEREMONT.
>   Sir, shall I lie?
KING.
>   Yes, lie and damn rather than tell me that.
>   I say again, where is she? Mutter not!
>   Sir, speak you; where is she? 25
DION.
>   Sir, I do not know.
KING.
>   Speak that again so boldly and by heaven
>   It is thy last. You fellows, answer me.
>   Where is she? Mark me, all; I am your king!
>   I wish to see my daughter. Show her me. 30
>   I do command you all, as you are subjects,
>   To show her me. What, am I not your king?
>   If ay, then am I not to be obey'd?
DION.
>   Yes, if you command things possible and honest.
KING.
>   Things possible and honest? Hear me, thou— 35
>   Thou traitor, that dar'st confine thy king to things
>   Possible and honest: show her me
>   Or let me perish if I cover not
>   All Sicily with blood!
DION.
>   Faith, I cannot unless you tell me where she is. 40
KING.
>   You have betray'd me. Y'have let me lose
>   The jewel of my life. Go bring her me
>   And set her here before me. 'Tis the king
>   Will have it so, whose breath can still the winds,

---

23. *damn*] "be damned" (*OED,* citing this passage).

IV.iv   PHILASTER

  Uncloud the sun, charm down the swelling sea,   45
  And stop the floods of heaven! Speak, can it not?
DION.
  No.
KING. No? Cannot the breath of kings do this?
DION.
  No, nor smell sweet itself if once the lungs
  Be but corrupted.
KING.   Is it so? Take heed.
DION.
  Sir, take you heed how you dare the powers   50
  That must be just.
KING.   Alas, what are we kings?
  Why do you gods place us above the rest
  To be serv'd, flatter'd, and ador'd till we
  Believe we hold within our hands your thunder;
  And when we come to try the power we have,   55
  There's not a leaf shakes at our threat'nings?
  I have sinn'd, 'tis true, and here stand to be punish'd,
  Yet would not thus be punish'd. Let me choose
  My way, and lay it on.
DION.
  He articles with the gods. Would somebody would draw   60
  bonds for the performance of covenants betwixt them!

    Enter Pharamond, Galatea, *and* Megra.

KING.
  What, is she found?
PHARAMOND.   No, we have ta'en her horse;
  He gallop'd empty by. There's some treason.
  You, Galatea, rode with her into the wood.
  Why left you her?
GALATEA.   She did command me.   65
KING.
  Command? You should not.

---

  60. *articles*] "to arrange by treaty, or stipulations" *(OED,* citing this passage).
  63. *empty*] riderless.
  63. *treason*] betrayal, breach of confidence, trickery.

GALATEA.
'Twould ill become my fortunes and my birth
To disobey the daughter of my king.
KING.
Y'are all cunning to obey us for our hurts.
But I will have her.
PHARAMOND. If I have her not, 70
By this hand there shall be no more Sicily.
DION [aside].
What, will he carry it to Spain in's pocket?
PHARAMOND.
I will not leave one man alive but the king,
A cook, and a tailor.
DION [aside].
Yes, you may do well to spare your lady bedfellow, and 75
her you may keep for a spawner.
KING [aside].
I see the injuries I have done must be reveng'd.
DION.
Sir, this is not the way to find her out.
KING.
Run all, disperse yourselves. The man that finds her
Or, if she be kill'd, the traitor, I'll make him great. 80
DION.
I know some would give five thousand pounds to find
her.
PHARAMOND.
Come, let us seek.
KING.
Each man a several way. Here, I myself.
DION.
Come, gentlemen, we here. 85
CLEREMONT.
Lady, you must go search, too.
MEGRA.
I had rather be search'd myself. *Exeunt omnes.*

---

76. *spawner*] obsolete term for a woman *(OED,* citing this passage); a derogatory name for one who reproduces.
84. *several*] separate, different.

IV.v   PHILASTER

[IV.v]   *Enter* Arethusa.

ARETHUSA.
    Where am I now? Feet, find me out a way
    Without the counsel of my troubled head.
    I'll follow you boldly about these woods,
    O'er mountains, through brambles, pits, and floods.
    Heaven I hope will ease me. I am sick.   [*Sits down.*]   5

          Enter Bellario.

BELLARIO.
    Yonder's my lady. God knows I want nothing
    Because I do not wish to live, yet I
    Will try her charity. Oh hear, you that have plenty;
    From that flowing store, drop some on dry ground. See,
    The lively red is gone to guard her heart.   10
    I fear she faints. Madam, look up! She breathes not.
    Open once more those rosy twins and send
    Unto my lord your latest farewell. Oh, she stirs!
    How is it, madam? Speak comfort.

ARETHUSA.
    'Tis not gently done   15
    To put me in a miserable life
    And hold me there. I prithee, let me go.
    I shall do best without thee. I am well.

          Enter Philaster.

PHILASTER [*aside*].
    I am to blame to be so much in rage.
    I'll tell her coolly when and where I heard   20
    This killing truth. I will be temperate
    In speaking and as just in hearing.—
    Oh, monstrous! Tempt me not, you gods; good gods,
    Tempt not a frail man! What's he that has a heart
    But he must ease it here?   25

BELLARIO.
    My lord, help! Help the princess.

---

12. *rosy twins*] red lips.

ARETHUSA.
    I am well. Forbear.
PHILASTER [*aside*].
    Let me love lightning, let me be embrac'd
    And kiss'd by scorpions, or adore the eyes
    Of basilisks rather than trust the tongues 30
    Of hell-bred woman. Some good god look down
    And shrink these veins up. Stick me here a stone
    Lasting to ages in the memory
    Of this damn'd act. —Hear me, you wicked ones!
    You have put hills of fire into this breast 35
    Not to be quench'd with tears, for which may guilt
    Sit on your bosoms. At your meals and beds
    Despair await you. What, before my face?
    Poison of asps between your lips! Diseases
    Be your best issues! Nature make a curse 40
    And throw it on you!
ARETHUSA.   Dear Philaster, leave
    To be enrag'd and hear me.
PHILASTER.   I have done.
    Forgive my passion. Not the calmed sea
    When Aeolus locks up his windy brood
    Is less disturb'd than I. I'll make you know't. 45
    Dear Arethusa, do but take this sword
    And search how temperate a heart I have.
    Then you and this your boy may live and reign
    In lust without control. Wilt thou, Bellario?
    I prithee, kill me. Thou art poor and may'st 50
    Nourish ambitious thoughts; when I am dead
    Thy way were freer. Am I raging now?
    If I were mad, I should desire to live.
    Sirs, feel my pulse; whether have you known
    A man in a more equal tune to die? 55

---

32. *Stick . . . stone*] erect here a monument.
44. *Aeolus*] classical god or king of the winds.
54. *Sirs*] "It should be recollected that *sir* was a term of address to females as well as men" (Weber).
54. *whether*] used without the alternative "or" to introduce a question.

IV.v   PHILASTER

BELLARIO.
　Alas, my lord, your pulse keeps madman's time.
　So does your tongue.
PHILASTER.   You will not kill me then?
ARETHUSA.
　Kill you!
BELLARIO.   Not for the world.
PHILASTER.   I blame not thee,
　Bellario. Thou hast done but that which gods
　Would have transform'd themselves to do. Be gone.   60
　Leave me without reply. This is the last
　Of all our meeting.   *Exit* Bellario.
　　　　　　　Kill me with this sword.
　Be wise, or worse will follow. We are two
　Earth cannot bear at once. Resolve to do,
　Or suffer.   65
ARETHUSA.
　If my fortune be so good to let me fall
　Upon thy hand, I shall have peace in death.
　Yet tell me this: there will be no slanders,
　No jealousy in the other world, no ill there?
PHILASTER.
　No.
ARETHUSA. Show me then the way.
PHILASTER.   Then guide   70
　My feeble hand, you that have power to do it,
　For I must perform a piece of justice. If your youth
　Have any way offended heaven, let prayers
　Short and effectual reconcile you to it.
ARETHUSA.
　I am prepar'd.   75

Enter a Country Fellow.

COUNTRY FELLOW.
　I'll see the king if he be in the forest. I have hunted him these two hours. If I should come home and not see him, my sisters would laugh at me. I can see nothing but people better hors'd than myself that outride me. I can hear nothing but shouting. These kings had need of   80

—80—

PHILASTER IV.v

good brains; this whooping is able to put a mean man
out of his wits. There's a courtier with his sword drawn;
by this hand, upon a woman, I think!

PHILASTER.
Are you at peace?

ARETHUSA.
With heaven and earth. 85

PHILASTER.
May they divide thy soul and body! [*Wounds her.*]

COUNTRY FELLOW.
Hold, dastard! Strike a woman! Thou'rt a craven; I
warrant thee, thou wouldst be loath to play half a dozen
venies at wasters with a good fellow for a broken head.

PHILASTER.
Leave us, good friend. 90

ARETHUSA.
What ill-bred man art thou, to intrude thyself
Upon our private sports, our recreations?

COUNTRY FELLOW.
God 'uds me, I understand you not, but I know the
rogue has hurt you.

PHILASTER.
Pursue thy own affairs. It will be ill 95
To multiply blood upon my head,
Which thou wilt force me to.

COUNTRY FELLOW.
I know not your rhetoric, but I can lay it on if you
touch the woman.   *They fight.*

PHILASTER.
Slave, take what thou deservest! 100

ARETHUSA.
Heaven guard my lord.

---

81. *mean*] of low degree; undistinguished in position; opposite of "noble" or "gentle" *(OED)*.
86. S.D. *Wounds her*] added by Weber and later editors; Q1, "Philaster *wounds her*" following l. 84.
89. *venies at wasters*] "bouts at cudgels" (Dyce).
93. *'uds*] judge (the Q1 reading).
96. *To . . . head*] to force me into more killings.
98. *rhetoric*] in the sense of elegant language.

—81—

IV.v PHILASTER

COUNTRY FELLOW.
 Oh, do you breathe?
PHILASTER.
 I hear the tread of people. I am hurt.
 The gods take part against me; could this boor
 Have held me thus else? I must shift for life 105
 Though I do loathe it. I would find a course
 To lose it rather by my will than force.   *Exit* Philaster.
COUNTRY FELLOW.
 I cannot follow the rogue. I pray thee, wench, come and kiss me now.

Enter Pharamond, Dion, *Cleremont, Thrasiline, and* Woodmen.

PHARAMOND.
 What art thou? 110
COUNTRY FELLOW.
 Almost kill'd I am for a foolish woman. A knave has hurt her.
PHARAMOND.
 The princess, gentlemen! Where's the wound, madam? Is it dangerous?
ARETHUSA.
 He has not hurt me. 115
COUNTRY FELLOW.
 By god, she lies. H'as hurt her in the breast. Look else.
PHARAMOND.
 Oh sacred spring of innocent blood!
DION.
 'Tis above wonder! Who should dare this?
ARETHUSA.
 I felt it not.
PHARAMOND.
 Speak, villain, who has hurt the princess? 120
COUNTRY FELLOW.
 Is it the princess?
DION.
 Ay.
COUNTRY FELLOW.
 Then I have seen something yet.

PHARAMOND.
  But who has hurt her?
COUNTRY FELLOW.
  I told you, a rogue. I ne'er saw him before, I.
PHARAMOND.
  Madam, who did it?
ARETHUSA.
  Some dishonest wretch. Alas, I know him not
  And do forgive him.
COUNTRY FELLOW.
  He's hurt, too. He cannot go far. I made my father's
  old fox fly about his ears.
PHARAMOND.
  How will you have me kill him?
ARETHUSA.
  Not at all. 'Tis some distracted fellow.
PHARAMOND.
  By this hand, I'll leave never a piece of him bigger than
  a nut and bring him all to you in my hat.
ARETHUSA.
  Nay, good sir,
  If you do take him, bring him quick to me
  And I will study for a punishment
  Great as his fault.
PHARAMOND.
  I will.
ARETHUSA.
  But swear.
PHARAMOND.
  By all my love, I will. Woodman, conduct the princess
  to the king and bear that wounded fellow to dressing.
  Come, gentlemen, we'll follow the chase close.

Exeunt Arethusa, Pharamond, Dion, *Cleremont, Thrasiline, and First Woodman.*

---

130. *old fox*] Old English broadsword (Dyce).
136. *quick*] alive.
142. *that wounded fellow*] the first clear indication that Philaster wounded the country fellow in their fight.

—83—

IV.v   PHILASTER

COUNTRY FELLOW.
    I pray you, friend, let me see the king.
2 WOODMAN.
    That you shall, and receive thanks.   145
COUNTRY FELLOW.
    If I get clear of this, I'll go to see no more gay sights.
                                                    Exeunt.

[IV.vi]   *Enter* Bellario.

BELLARIO.
    A heaviness near death sits on my brow,
    And I must sleep. Bear me, thou gentle bank,
    Forever if thou wilt. You sweet ones all,
    Let me unworthy press you. I could wish
    I rather were a corse strew'd o'er with you   5
    Than quick above you. Dullness shuts mine eyes,
    And I am giddy. Oh that I could take
    So sound a sleep that I might never wake!

                      Enter Philaster.

PHILASTER.
    I have done ill; my conscience calls me false,
    To strike at her that would not strike at me.   10
    When I did fight, methought I heard her pray
    The gods to guard me. She may be abus'd
    And I a loathed villain. If she be,
    She will conceal who hurt her. He has wounds
    And cannot follow; neither knows he me.   15
    Who's this? Bellario sleeping! If thou beest
    Guilty, there is no justice that thy sleep
    Should be so sound and mine, whom thou hast wrong'd,
    So broken.   *Cry within.*
          Hark, I am pursu'd. You gods,
    I'll take this offer'd means of my escape.   20
    They have no mark to know me but my wounds,
    If she be true. If false, let mischief light

---

5. *corse*] corpse.

PHILASTER								IV.vi

On all the world at once. Sword, print my wounds
Upon this sleeping boy. I ha' none, I think,
Are mortal, nor would I lay greater on thee.				25
							Wounds him.
BELLARIO.
Oh, death I hope is come! Blest be that hand;
It meant me well. Again, for pity's sake.
PHILASTER.
I have caught myself.				Philaster *falls.*
The loss of blood hath stay'd my flight. Here, here
Is he that struck thee. Take thy full revenge.				30
Use me, as I did mean thee, worse than death.
I'll teach thee to revenge. This luckless hand
Wounded the princess. Tell my followers
Thou didst receive these hurts in staying me
And I will second thee. Get a reward.				35
BELLARIO.
Fly, fly, my lord, and save yourself!
PHILASTER.				How's this?
Wouldst thou I should be safe?
BELLARIO.				Else were it vain
For me to live. These little wounds I have
Ha' not bled much. Reach me that noble hand.
I'll help to cover you.
PHILASTER.				Art thou true to me?				40
BELLARIO.
Or let me perish loath'd! Come, my good lord,
Creep in among those bushes. Who does know
But that the gods may save your much lov'd breath?
PHILASTER.
Then I shall die for grief, if not for this,
That I have wounded thee. What wilt thou do?				45

---

31. *mean thee*] mean to use thee.
33. *followers*] pursuers *(OED).*
35. *Get a reward*] A line may have been dropped at this point in the Q2 text (Turner notes this possibility); there is a comma after *reward*, the last word on sig. H4ᵛ, and the catchword is *And.* The next line, at the top of sig. I1, is Bellario's speech *Fly, fly, my lord.*

—85—

IV.vi   PHILASTER

BELLARIO.
  Shift for myself well. Peace, I hear 'em come.
                              [Philaster *hides*.]
WITHIN.
  Follow, follow, follow! That way they went.
BELLARIO.
  With my own wounds I'll bloody my own sword.
  I need not counterfeit to fall. Heaven knows
  That I can stand no longer.   50

    Enter Pharamond, Dion, Cleremont, *Thrasiline*.

PHARAMOND.
  To this place we have track'd him by his blood.
CLEREMONT.
  Yonder, my lord, creeps one away.
DION.
  Stay, sir, what are you?
BELLARIO.
  A wretched creature wounded in these woods
  By beasts. Relieve me, if your names be men,   55
  Or I shall perish.
DION.   This is he, my lord,
  Upon my soul, that hurt her. 'Tis the boy,
  That wicked boy that serv'd her.
PHARAMOND.
  Oh, thou damn'd in thy creation!
  What cause couldst thou shape to strike the princess? 60
BELLARIO.
  Then I am betray'd.
DION.
  Betray'd! No; apprehended.
BELLARIO.   I confess;
  Urge it no more that, big with evil thoughts,
  I set upon her and did make my aim
  Her death. For charity, let fall at once   65
  The punishment you mean and do not load
  This weary flesh with tortures.
PHARAMOND.
  I will know who hir'd thee to this deed.

—86—

BELLARIO.
　Mine own revenge.
PHARAMOND.
　Revenge, for what?
BELLARIO.　　　　It pleas'd her to receive　　　　70
　Me as her page, and when my fortunes ebb'd
　That men strid o'er them careless, she did shower
　Her welcome graces on me and did swell
　My fortunes till they overflow'd their banks,
　Threat'ning the men that cross'd 'em; when, as swift　75
　As storms arise at sea, she turn'd her eyes
　To burning suns upon me and did dry
　The streams she had bestow'd, leaving me worse
　And more contemn'd than other little brooks
　Because I had been great. In short, I knew　　　80
　I could not live and therefore did desire
　To die reveng'd.
PHARAMOND.　　　　If tortures can be found
　Long as thy natural life, resolve to feel
　The utmost rigor.
CLEREMONT.　　　　Help to lead him hence.
　　　　　　　　　Philaster *creeps out of a bush.*
PHILASTER.
　Turn back, you ravishers of innocence.　　　　85
　Know ye the price of that you bear away
　So rudely?
PHARAMOND.　Who's that?
DION.　　　　　'Tis the lord Philaster.
PHILASTER.
　'Tis not the treasure of all kings in one,
　The wealth of Tagus, nor the rocks of pearl
　That pave the court of Neptune, can weigh down　90
　That virtue. It was I that hurt the princess.
　Place me, some god, upon a pyramis

---

89. *Tagus*] river in Spain and Portugal; sometimes used as a symbol of Spain, as in Sir Thomas Wyatt's epigram "Tagus Farewell."
90. *Neptune*] Greek god of the sea.
92. *pyramis*] pyramid.

IV.vi   PHILASTER

  Higher than hills of earth and lend a voice
  Loud as your thunder to me, that from thence
  I may discourse to all the under-world   95
  The worth that dwells in him.
PHARAMOND.   How's this?
BELLARIO.   My lord, some man
  Weary of life that would be glad to die.
PHILASTER.
  Leave these untimely courtesies, Bellario.
BELLARIO.
  Alas, he's mad. Come, will you lead me on?
PHILASTER.
  By all the oaths that men ought most to keep 100
  And gods do punish most when men do break,
  He touch'd her not! Take heed, Bellario,
  How thou dost drown the virtues thou hast shown
  With perjury. By all the gods, 'twas I!
  You know she stood betwixt me and my right. 105
PHARAMOND.
  Thy own tongue be thy judge.
CLEREMONT.
  It was Philaster.
DION.   Is't not a brave boy?
  Well, sirs, I fear me we were all deceiv'd.
PHILASTER.
  Have I no friend here?
DION.   Yes.
PHILASTER.   Then show it.
  Some good body lend a hand to draw us nearer. 110
  Would you have tears shed for you when you die?
  Then lay me gently on his neck, that there
  I may weep floods and breathe forth my spirit.
  'Tis not the wealth of Plutus nor the gold
  Lock'd in the heart of earth, can buy away 115
  This armful from me. This had been a ransom
  To have redeem'd the great Augustus Caesar
  Had he been taken. You hard-hearted men,

---

114. *Plutus*] Roman allegorical figure standing for Wealth.

PHILASTER   IV.vi

More stony than these mountains, can you see
Such clear, pure blood drop and not cut your flesh   120
To stop his life? To bind whose bitter wounds
Queens ought to tear their hair and with their tears
Bathe 'em. Forgive me, thou that art the wealth
Of poor Philaster.

     Enter King, Arethusa, *and a guard.*

KING.
  Is the villain ta'en?
PHARAMOND.   Sir, here be two   125
  Confess the deed, but sure it was Philaster.
PHILASTER.
  Question it no more; it was.
KING.
  The fellow that did fight with him will tell us that.
ARETHUSA.
  Ay me, I know he will.
KING.   Did not you know him?
ARETHUSA.
  Sir, if it was he, he was disguised.   130
PHILASTER.
  I was so. Oh my stars, that I should live still!
KING.
  Thou ambitious fool,
  Thou that hast laid a train for thy own life!
  Now I do mean to do; I'll leave to talk.
  Bear them to prison.   135
ARETHUSA.
  Sir, they did plot together to take hence
  This harmless life. Should it pass unreveng'd,
  I should to earth go weeping. Grant me, then,
  By all the love a father bears his child,
  Their custodies, and that I may appoint   140
  Their tortures and their deaths.

---

121. *stop*] probably in the sense of stanch, as a wound draining life-blood.

126. *sure*] Q2–9 and F read *say*; Q1 has *sute*. Dyce and most later editors emend to *sure*.

IV.vi   PHILASTER

DION.
　Death! Soft, our law will not reach that, for this fault.
KING.
　'Tis granted. Take 'em to you, with a guard.
　Come, princely Pharamond, this business past
　We may with more security go on   145
　To your intended match.
CLEREMONT.
　I pray that this action lose not Philaster the hearts of the people.
DION.
　Fear it not. Their overwise heads will think it but a trick.   *Exeunt omnes.* 150

[V.i]   *Enter* Dion, Cleremont, *and* Thrasiline.

THRASILINE.
　Has the king sent for him to death?
DION.
　Yes, but the king must know 'tis not in his power to war with heaven.
CLEREMONT.
　We linger time. The king sent for Philaster and the headsman an hour ago.   5
THRASILINE.
　Are all his wounds well?
DION.
　All. They were but scratches, but the loss of blood made him faint.
CLEREMONT.
　We dally, gentlemen.
THRASILINE.
　Away.   10
DION.
　We'll scuffle hard before he perish.   *Exeunt.*

---

　1. *to death*] to be put to death.
　4. *linger*] prolong, protract, draw out *(OED)*.

PHILASTER V.ii

[V.ii] *Enter* Philaster, Arethusa, Bellario [*in prison*].

ARETHUSA.
 Nay, faith, Philaster, grieve not. We are well.
BELLARIO.
 Nay, good my lord, forbear. We're wondrous well.
PHILASTER.
 Oh, Arethusa! Oh, Bellario! Leave to be kind.
 I shall be shut from heaven as now from earth
 If you continue so. I am a man 5
 False to a pair of the most trusty ones
 That ever earth bore. Can it bear us all?
 Forgive and leave me. But the king hath sent
 To call me to my death. Oh, show it me
 And then forget me! And for thee, my boy, 10
 I shall deliver words will mollify
 The hearts of beasts to spare thy innocence.
BELLARIO.
 Alas, my lord, my life is not a thing
 Worthy your noble thoughts. 'Tis not a life,
 'Tis but a piece of childhood thrown away. 15
 Should I outlive you, I should then outlive
 Virtue and honor. And when that day comes,
 If ever I shall close these eyes but once,
 May I live spotted for my perjury
 And waste by limbs to nothing. 20
ARETHUSA.
 And I, the woeful'st maid that ever was,
 Forc'd with my hands to bring my lord to death,
 Do by the honor of a virgin swear
 To tell no hours beyond it.
PHILASTER.
 Make me not hated so. 25

---

4. *shut*] the Q1 reading, followed by Dyce and most later editors. Turner follows Q2 *shot* (i.e., expelled). *Shut* seems the better reading because of the prison connotation.

20. *by limbs*] the Q2 reading, followed by Dyce. Q1 reads *by time*, followed by Daniel. Turner adopts the Q3 reading *my limbs*.

24. *tell*] count.

—91—

ARETHUSA.
    Come from this prison all joyful to our deaths.
PHILASTER.
    People will tear me when they find you true
    To such a wretch as I. I shall die loath'd.
    Enjoy your kingdoms peaceably whilst I
    Forever sleep, forgotten with my faults.   30
    Every just servant, every maid in love,
    Will have a piece of me if you be true.
ARETHUSA.
    My dear lord, say not so.
BELLARIO.   A piece of you?
    He was not born of woman that can cut it
    And look on.
PHILASTER.   Take me in tears betwixt you,   35
    For my heart will break with shame and sorrow.
ARETHUSA.
    Why, 'tis well.
BELLARIO.
    Lament no more.
PHILASTER.   What would you have done
    If you had wrong'd me basely and had found
    Your life no price, compar'd to mine? For love, sirs,   40
    Deal with me truly.
BELLARIO.   'Twas mistaken, sir.
PHILASTER.
    Why, if it were?
BELLARIO.
    Then, sir, we would have ask'd your pardon.
PHILASTER.
    And have hope to enjoy it?
ARETHUSA.   Enjoy it? Ay.
PHILASTER.
    Would you indeed? Be plain.

---

31. *servant*] lover.
40. *Your life . . . mine*] Q1–9 and F read *my life . . . yours*. The transposition in the present text was suggested by Mason, followed by Weber and most later editors.

PHILASTER V.iii

BELLARIO. We would, my lord. 45
PHILASTER.
  Forgive me, then.
ARETHUSA. So, so.
BELLARIO.
  'Tis as it should be now.
PHILASTER. Lead to my death. *Exeunt.*

[V.iii] *Enter* King, Dion, Cleremont, Thrasiline.

KING.
  Gentlemen, who saw the prince?
CLEREMONT.
  So please you, sir, he's gone to see the city
  And the new platform, with some gentlemen
  Attending on him.
KING. Is the princess ready
  To bring her prisoner out?
THRASILINE. She waits, your grace. 5
KING.
  Tell her we stay.
DION [*aside*].
  King, you may be deceiv'd yet.
  The head you aim at cost more setting on
  Than to be lost so lightly. If it must off
  Like a wild overflow that soops before him 10
  A golden stack and with it shakes down bridges,

---

3. *platform*] J. E. Savage ("The 'Gaping Wounds' in the Text of *Philaster*," *Philological Quarterly*, XXVIII [1949], 443–457), finds an allusion to a platform used by King James I on May 8, 1609, to hear charges of mismanagement against the navy, especially in the construction of a large ship for Prince Henry; the platform, according to Savage, "was built apparently as a replica of a warship's deck, to clarify technical matters on ship measurements" (pp. 453–454). James dismissed the charges.

6. *stay*] remain, wait.

10. *soops*] swoops *(OED)*; many modern editors emend to *swoops*, although Daniel and Turner retain *soops*, the reading of all early editions.

—93—

V.iii　　　　　　　　　　PHILASTER

    Cracks the strong hearts of pines whose cable roots
    Held out a thousand storms, a thousand thunders,
    And, so made mightier, takes whole villages
    Upon his back and in that heat of pride　　　　15
    Charges strong towns, towers, castles, palaces,
    And lays them desolate; so shall thy head,
    Thy noble head, bury the lives of thousands
    That must bleed with thee like a sacrifice
    In thy red ruins.　　　　20

Enter Philaster, Arethusa, Bellario *in a robe and garland.*

KING.
    How now, what masque is this?
BELLARIO.
    Right royal sir, I should
    Sing you an epithalamion of these lovers;
    But having lost my best airs with my fortunes
    And wanting a celestial harp to strike　　　　25
    This blessed union on, thus in glad story
    I give you all. These two fair cedar branches,
    The noblest of the mountain, where they grew
    Straightest and tallest, under whose still shades
    The worthier beasts have made their lairs and slept　　　　30
    Free from the fervor of the Sirian star
    And the fell thunder-stroke, free from the clouds
    When they were big with humor and deliver'd
    In thousand spouts their issues to the earth;
    Oh, there was none but silent quiet there,　　　　35
    Till never-pleased Fortune shot up shrubs,
    Base underbrambles, to divorce these branches.

---

    21. *masque*] dramatic entertainment popular at court, offering elaborate music, dancing, and costumes.
    23. *epithalamion*] type of lyric poem celebrating a wedding.
    24. *airs*] melodies, tunes.
    31. *the fervor of . . . star*] Only Q1 of the early texts reads *the fervor of* the Sirian star; editors since Dyce have added these three words to the Q2 text. The reference is to the Dog-star Sirius; cf. IV.i.47 (Dog-days).
    33. *humor*] moisture, vapor *(OED)*.

And for awhile they did so and did reign
Over the mountain and choke up his beauty
With brakes, rude thorns, and thistles till the sun 40
Scorch'd them even to the roots and dried them there.
And now a gentler gale hath blown again
That made these branches meet and twine together,
Never to be divided. The god that sings
His holy numbers over marriage beds 45
Hath knit their noble hearts and here they stand,
Your children, mighty king; and I have done.
KING.
How, how?
ARETHUSA.   Sir, if you love it in plain truth,
For now there is no masquing in't, this gentleman,
The prisoner that you gave me, is become 50
My keeper, and through all the bitter throes
Your jealousies and his ill fate have wrought him,
Thus nobly hath he struggled and at length
Arrived here my dear husband.
KING.
Your dear husband! Call in 55
The captain of the citadel. There you shall keep
Your wedding. I'll provide a masque shall make
Your Hymen turn his saffron into a sullen coat
And sing sad requiems to your departing souls.
Blood shall put out your torches, and instead 60
Of gaudy flowers about your wanton necks,
An axe shall hang like a prodigious meteor
Ready to crop your love's sweets. Hear, you gods!
From this time do I shake all title off
Of father to this woman, this base woman; 65
And what there is of vengeance in a lion
Chaf'd among dogs or robb'd of his dear young,
The same enforc'd more terrible, more mighty,
Expect from me.

---

58. *Your Hymen . . . coat*] Hymen, Greek god of marriage, "was always appropriately clothed in saffron-coloured robes in the ancient masques and pageantries" (Weber).

62. *prodigious*] ominous, portentous *(OED)*.

V.iii   PHILASTER

ARETHUSA.
    Sir, by that little life I have left to swear by,   70
    There's nothing that can stir me from myself.
    What I have done, I have done without repentance,
    For death can be no bugbear unto me
    So long as Pharamond is not my headsman.
DION [aside].
    Sweet peace upon thy soul, thou worthy maid,   75
    Whene'er thou diest! For this time I'll excuse thee
    Or be thy prologue.
PHILASTER.   Sir, let me speak next,
    And let my dying words be better with you
    Than my dull living actions. If you aim
    At the dear life of this sweet innocent,   80
    Y'are a tyrant and a savage monster.
    Your memory shall be as foul behind you
    As you are living. All your better deeds
    Shall be in water writ, but this in marble.
    No chronicle shall speak you, though your own,   85
    But for the shame of men. No monument,
    Though high and big as Pelion, shall be able
    To cover this base murder. Make it rich
    With brass, with purest gold and shining jasper
    Like the pyramids, lay on epitaphs   90
    Such as make great men gods; my little marble
    That only clothes my ashes, not my faults,
    Shall far outshine it. And for after-issues,
    Think not so madly of the heavenly wisdom
    That they will give you more for your mad rage   95
    To cut off, unless it be some snake or something

---

    73. *bugbear*] hobgoblin.
    77. *prologue*] speech introducing and explaining the action of a play; frequently employed by Elizabethan and Jacobean playwrights.
    81. *Y'are . . . monster*] Q1 adds the line *That feeds upon the blood you gave a life to;* adopted into the text by Dyce and later editors.
    85. *chronicle*] history, annals.
    87. *Pelion*] mountain in Thessaly which figured in the legendary struggle of the giants against the Greek gods.
    93. *after-issues*] progeny.

Like yourself, that in his birth shall strangle you.
Remember my father, king. There was a fault,
But I forgive it. Let that sin persuade you
To love this lady. If you have a soul, 100
Think, save her, and be sav'd. For myself,
I have so long expected this glad hour,
So languish'd under you and daily wither'd,
That by the gods it is a joy to die.
I find a recreation in't. 105

Enter a Messenger.

MESSENGER.
 Where's the king?
KING.   Here.
MESSENGER.   Get you to your strength
 And rescue the prince Pharamond from danger.
 He's taken prisoner by the citizens,
 Fearing the lord Philaster.
DION [*aside*].   Oh brave followers!
 Mutiny, my fine dear countrymen, mutiny! 110
 Now, my brave valiant foremen, show your weapons
 In honor of your mistresses!

Enter another Messenger.

2 MESSENGER.
 Arm, arm, arm, arm!
KING.
 A thousand devils take 'em.
DION [*aside*].
 A thousand blessings on 'em. 115
2 MESSENGER.
 Arm, oh king! The city is in mutiny,
 Led by an old gray ruffian who comes on
 In rescue of the lord Philaster.
KING.
 Away to the citadel.

---

109. *Fearing*] fearing for (Dyce).
111. *foremen*] chief or leading men; also the front rank of men in a military engagement *(OED)*.

V.iii   PHILASTER

Exit with Arethusa, Philaster, Bellario.

I'll see them safe
And then cope with these burghers. Let the guard   120
And all the gentlemen give strong attendance.   *Exit* King.

Manent Dion, Cleremont, Thrasiline.

CLEREMONT.
The city up! This was above our wishes.
DION.
Ay, and the marriage, too. By my life, this noble lady
has deceiv'd us all. A plague upon myself, a thousand
plagues, for having such unworthy thoughts of her dear 125
honor. Oh, I could beat myself; or do you beat me and
I'll beat you, for we had all one thought.
CLEREMONT.
No, no, 'twill but lose time.
DION.
You say true. Are your swords sharp? Well, my dear
countrymen what-ye-lacks, if you continue and fall not 130
back upon the first broken shin, I'll have ye chronicled
and chronicled, and cut and chronicled, and all-to-be-
prais'd and sung in sonnets and bath'd in new brave
ballads, that all tongues shall troul you *in secula seculorum,* my kind can-carriers.   135

---

120. *burghers*] citizens; inhabitants of a town or borough.
121.1. *Manent*] They remain; Dyce's direction reads, *"Exeunt all except* Dion, Cleremont, *and* Thrasiline."
130. *what-ye-lacks*] "i.e. shopkeepers, —'what do you lack,' being formerly the usual address of the London shopkeepers to the passers by" (Dyce).
132. *cut*] "to carve, represent in stone" (Onions).
133. *bath'd*] suffused, encompassed, enveloped *(OED)*. Theobald emends to *graved,* Dyce to *bawled.* The present reading, followed by Turner, stands in all early editions.
134. *troul*] troll, to sing, especially in successive parts as a catch or round *(OED)*.
134–135. *in secula seculorum*] "to the ages of ages, to all eternity, for ever and ever" *(OED,* citing Peele's use in *Edward I* "To follow my fortune in *secula seculorum"*).
135. *can-carriers*] literally, carriers of vessels used for drinking *(OED* cites this passage).

PHILASTER V.iii

THRASILINE.

What if a toy take 'em i'th' heels now, and they run all away and cry, "The devil take the hindmost"?

DION.

Then the same devil take the foremost, too, and souse him for his breakfast. If they all prove cowards, my curses fly among them and be speeding. May they have 140 murrains reign to keep the gentlemen at home unbound in easy frieze. May the moths branch their velvets, and their silks only be worn before sore eyes. May their false lights undo 'em and discover presses, holes, stains, and oldness in their stuffs and make them shoprid. May they 145 keep whores and horses, and break, and live mew'd up with necks of beef and turnips. May they have many children, and none like the father. May they know no language but that gibberish they prattle to their parcels, unless it be the goatish Latin they write in their bonds, 150 and may they write that false and lose their debts.

---

136. *toy*] "a foolish or idle fancy . . . a whim" *(OED)*.

138. *souse*] drench in liquid, usually for pickling.

141. *murrains*] plagues, pestilence.

142. *frieze*] "kind of coarse woollen cloth" *(OED)*.

142. *branch*] "adorn or embroider with gold or needlework representing flowers or foliage" *(OED,* citing this passage and a similar usage at V.iv.38). The moths, of course, are "embroidering" in the sense of eating away parts of the velvet.

143. *silks . . . eyes*] *OED* cites a similar passage in Shakespeare's *Troilus and Cressida* (V.1.36): "Thou green sarcenet [silk] flap for a sore eye." *Before* in the present passage is used in the sense of "in front of" or "over."

143–144. *false lights*] "Were used, it would seem, in the shops of dishonest London tradesmen, to enable them to palm upon their customers injured or inferior goods" (Dyce).

145. *stuffs*] fabrics.

146. *break*] "to become bankrupt, to 'fail' (commercially)" *(OED)*.

146. *mew'd up*] closed up, as in a cage.

147. *necks of beef*] "Neck-beef" denotes meat of inferior quality *(OED)*, here probably beef stewed with turnips.

149. *parcels*] small party or company; group, set; often used contemptuously *(OED)*.

150. *goatish Latin*] Theobald emends to "gothic," but Dyce points out that "goatish," like gothic, can mean rank, coarse, barbarous.

V.iii PHILASTER

Enter the King.

KING.

Now the vengeance of all the gods confound them. How they swarm together! What a hum they raise! Devils choke your wild throats. If a man had need to use their valors, he must pay a brokage for it, and then bring 155 'em on and they will fight like sheep. 'Tis Philaster, none but Philaster, must allay this heat. They will not hear me speak, but fling dirt at me and call me tyrant. Oh run, dear friend, and bring the lord Philaster! Speak him fair, call him prince, do him all the courtesy you 160 can. Commend me to him. Oh my wits, my wits!

Exit Cleremont.

DION [*aside*].

Oh my brave countrymen! As I live, I will not buy a pin out of your walls for this. Nay, you shall cozen me, and I'll thank you and send you brawn and bacon, and soil you every long vacation a brace of foremen that at 165 Michaelmas shall come up fat and kicking.

KING.

What they will do with this poor prince the gods know and I fear.

DION.

Why, sir, they'll flay him and make church buckets on's skin to quench rebellion, then clap a rivet in's sconce 170 and hang him up for a sign.

Enter Cleremont *with* Philaster.

---

155. *brokage*] brokerage, a broker's commission or premium *(OED)*.
162-163. *not buy . . . walls*] not buy even a trifling item outside your shops, in gratitude for the citizens' help. Hazelton Spencer *(Elizabethan Plays,* 1933 ed.) suggests *outside the city* for *out of your walls.*
163. *cozen*] defraud, trick.
164. *brawn*] usually boar's flesh, often pickled or potted *(OED).*
165. *soil*] "to feed up or fatten (fowls)" *(OED,* citing this passage).
165. *foremen*] "can only be a sort of cant name for geese" (Dyce).
166. *Michaelmas*] the feast of Saint Michael, September 29.
169. *church buckets*] "kept in the parish church for use in case of fire" *(OED,* citing this passage).
170. *sconce*] "jocular term for the head" *(OED).*

PHILASTER V.iv

KING.
Oh, worthy sir, forgive me. Do not make
Your miseries and my faults meet together
To bring a greater danger. Be yourself,
Still sound amongst diseases. I have wrong'd you, 175
And though I find it last and beaten to it,
Let first your goodness know it. Calm the people,
And be what you were born to. Take your love
And with her my repentance, all my wishes,
And all my prayers. By the gods, my heart speaks this; 180
And if the least fall from me not perform'd,
May I be struck with thunder!
PHILASTER. Mighty sir,
I will not do your greatness so much wrong
As not to make your word truth. Free the princess
And the poor boy, and let me stand the shock 185
Of this mad sea-breach, which I'll either turn
Or perish with it.
KING. Let your own word free them.
PHILASTER.
Then thus I take my leave, kissing your hand
And hanging on your royal word. Be kingly,
And be not mov'd, sir. I shall bring you peace 190
Or never bring myself back.
KING.
All the gods go with thee. *Exeunt omnes.*

[V.iv] *Enter an old* Captain *and* Citizens *with* Pharamond.

CAPTAIN.
Come, my brave myrmidons, let's fall on. Let your caps
swarm, my boys, and your nimble tongues forget your
mother gibberish of what-do-you-lack; and set your

---

186. *sea-breach*] Breach refers to heavy surf breaking over rocks *(OED)*; here the turbulent waters so formed.
[V.iv]
1. *myrmidons*] "one of a warlike race of men inhabiting ancient Thessaly, whom, according to the Homeric story, Achilles led to the siege of Troy" *(OED)*.
3. *what-do-you-lack*] see V.iii.130, note.

—101—

V.iv   PHILASTER

    mouths ope, children, till your palates fall frighted half
a fathom, past the cure of bay-salt and gross pepper, and   5
then cry "Philaster, brave Philaster!" Let Philaster be
deeper in request, my ding-dongs, my pairs of dear
indentures, kings of clubs, than your cold water camlets
or your paintings spitted with copper. Let not your
hasty silks or your branch'd cloth of bodkin, or your   10
tissues, dearly belov'd of spic'd cake and custards, your
Robin Hoods, Scarlets and Johns, tie your affections in
darkness to your shops. No, dainty duckers. Up with
your three-pil'd spirits, your wrought valors, and let your

---

  5. *bay-salt*] "salt, obtained in large crystals by slow evaporation; originally, from sea-water by the sun's heat" *(OED)*.

  5. *gross pepper*] coarsely ground; sometimes suggestive of inferior *(OED)*.

  7. *ding-dongs*] or ding-dings, an obsolete expression of endearment *(OED,* citing this passage).

  8. *indentures*] apprentices or servants bound to service by certificates of indenture.

  8. *kings of clubs*] "Clubs were formerly the favorite weapons of the London shopkeepers, which, when a fray arose in the streets, their apprentices were always ready to use" (Dyce).

  8. *camlets*] originally, costly Eastern fabrics; later, material of varied substance, usually Angora goat's hair in the sixteenth century. Watered or water camlet had a wavy surface *(OED)*.

  9. *spitted*] interwoven, in imitation of fabrics so treated with gold and silver thread; *paintings* probably means "painted cloths" (Daniel).

  10. *hasty silks*] "Must mean, I presume, loaded with paste or other material to give them false substance" (Daniel).

  10. *branched . . . bodkin*] "Embroidered or figured cloth of gold and silk" (Daniel).

  11. *your*] the reading of all early editions; some editors (e.g., Daniel, Turner) adopt Theobald's emendation "you."

  12. *Robin Hoods . . . Johns*] Robin Hood, Will Scarlet, and Little John, as members of the legendary band of English folk heroes in Sherwood Forest, were especially popular with apprentices and ordinary citizens.

  13. *duckers*] "i.e. cringers, bowers—alluding to their *ducking* (bowing) to customers" (Dyce). Daniel suggests that the allusion is more probably to duck-hunting, a popular sport with the citizens.

  14. *three-pil'd*] "three-pile was velvet of the richest and strongest quality" (Dyce).

  14. *valors*] a pun on "velour" or "velure," velvet-like.

uncut cholers make the king feel the measure of your 15
mightiness. Philaster! Cry, my rose-nobles, cry!

ALL.
Philaster, Philaster!

CAPTAIN.
How do you like this, my lord prince? These are mad
boys, I tell you; these are things that will not strike
their top-sails to a foist and let a man-of-war, an argosy, 20
hull and cry cockles.

PHARAMOND.
Why, you rude slave, do you know what you do?

CAPTAIN.
My pretty prince of puppets, we do know and give your
greatness warning that you talk no more such bug-words,
or that solder'd crown shall be scratch'd with a musket. 25

---

15. *cholers*] a pun on "collars," part of a man's dress, and "cholers," anger. Dyce and most later editors emend the Q2 spelling *collers* to *cholers*.

16. *rose-nobles*] gold coins of the fifteenth and sixteenth centuries; a variety of the noble stamped with a rose *(OED)*.

20. *foist*] "a small vessel, a pleasure-boat" (Daniel). Weber notes that *foist* refers to Pharamond and *man-of-war, an argosy* (a large vessel) to Philaster.

21. *hull and cry cockles*] *Hull* means to float or drift with sails furled; the phrase "to cry cock" means to acknowledge someone as victor *(OED)*. A "cockle" is a small, shallow boat shaped like a cockle-shell. Thus there may be a pun on "cockles-cock." The entire phrase means that the citizens are unwilling to see Philaster give in to Pharamond. J. E. Savage believes there is a reference here to the launching on September 24, 1610, of the large ship built at Woolwich for Prince Henry (see V.iii.3 note). "Prince Henry was to ride the ship down the ways, and when she floated, to christen her the 'Prince Royal.' But the tide was insufficient, and . . . 'the ship settled so hard upon the ground that there was no possibility of launching that tide.'" (Savage, "Gaping Wounds," p. 455). Savage notes that the possible Q2 allusion to this royal misfortune is softened in Q1 from *hull and cry cockles* to *stoop to carry coals* (do degrading work).

24. *bug-words*] "i.e. swaggering, high-sounding words,—properly, terrific words, from *bug*, a goblin" (Dyce).

25. *solder'd crown*] Daniel suggests "head" for *crown* but is at a loss to explain *solder'd*. The captain may be referring contemptuously to Pharamond's claim to a crown, through his betrothal to Arethusa,

V.iv PHILASTER

Dear prince pippin, down with your noble blood or, as
I live, I'll have you coddl'd. Let 'im loose, my spirits.
Make us a round ring with your bills, my Hectors, and
let me see what this trim man dares do. Now, sir, have
at you! Here I lie, and with this washing blow do you   30
see, sweet prince, I could hulk your grace and hang you
up cross-legg'd like a hare at a poulter's, and do this with
this wiper.

PHARAMOND.
You will not see me murder'd, wicked villains?
1 CITIZEN.
Yes indeed will we, sir. We have not seen one for a   35
great while.

---

as being patched together like soldered metal. *OED* cites this use in Fletcher's *Bloody Brother,* II.i: "A solder'd friendship Piec'd out with promises."

25. *musket*] "a male sparrow-hawk" (Dyce); but the pun involves a hint that Pharamond may have his brains blown out (Daniel).

26. *pippin*] literally, an apple; used in slang to apply to people, often with a derogatory connotation.

27. *coddl'd*] boiled, stewed; especially fruit, as suggested by *pippin* (*OED,* citing this passage).

28. *bills*] halberds; weapons varying in form from a blade with a long wooden handle to a kind of spiked ax with a spearheaded shaft. A similar weapon was used by constables of the watch as late as the eighteenth century (*OED*).

28. *Hectors*] heroes, like Hector of Troy; often by the mid-seventeenth century connoting bullies (those who "hector" others), though perhaps not in this passage.

29. *trim*] ironically used as fine, nice, pretty (*OED*).

30. *washing*] the reading of Q1 and Q2; Q3–9, F, and most editors except Turner, *swashing*. *OED* cites *washing* as a synonym for *swashing* when used to describe a forceful blow. The present passage is cited in *OED* as an example of the use of *swashing* because that reading presumably appears in editions of *Philaster* used by *OED* compilers.

31. *hulk*] so Q3–9, F, and most editors except Dyce, Daniel, who follow the Q1 reading *hock* (to hamstring). *Hulk* means to disembowel (*OED,* citing this passage).

33. *wiper*] slang for a person or a thing that strikes or assails; here a weapon (*OED,* citing this passage). With this line, correspondence between the Q1 and Q2 texts ceases, except for several stage directions in Q1 suggesting similar action.

CAPTAIN.

> He would have weapons, would he? Give him a broadside, my brave boys, with your pikes. Branch me his skin in flowers like a satin, and between every flower a mortal cut. Your royalty shall ravel. Jag him, gentlemen. I'll 40 have him cut to the kell, then down the seams. Oh for a whip to make him galloon-laces! I'll have a coach whip.

PHARAMOND.

> Oh spare me, gentlemen!

CAPTAIN.

> Hold, hold. The man begins to fear and know himself. He shall for this time only be seel'd up with a feather 45 through his nose, that he may only see heaven and think whither he's going. Nay, my beyond-sea sir, we will proclaim you: you would be king. Thou tender heir-apparent to a church-ale, thou slight prince of single sarcenet, thou royal ring-tail, fit to fly at nothing but 50 poor men's poultry and have every boy beat thee from that, too, with his bread and butter.

PHARAMOND.

> Gods keep me from these hellhounds!

1 CITIZEN.

> Shall's geld him, Captain?

37–38. *broadside*] a volley, as the discharge of guns from one side of a fighting vessel.

38. *Branch*] See earlier usage at V.iii.142.

40. *Jag*] "to pierce with a sharp instrument, to stab" *(OED,* citing this passage).

41. *kell*] "fatty membrane investing the intestines; the omentum; caul" *(OED,* citing this passage).

42. *galloon*] "narrow, close-woven ribbon or braid . . . used for trimming articles of apparel" *(OED,* citing this passage).

45. *seel'd*] term in falconry for closing a bird's eyes by stitching with thread *(OED);* at times a small feather was used (Dyce).

49. *church-ale*] "periodical festive gathering held in connexion with a church" *(OED).* Daniel notes: "In view of the enormities said . . . to be perpetrated at these festivals this may be considered as equivalent to being called a bastard."

50. *sarcenet*] or sarsenet; "very fine and soft silk material" *(OED).*

50. *ring-tail*] an inferior member of the falcon family, with whitish feathers on the tail (Daniel); female of the hen-harrier, once considered a distinct species *(OED,* citing this passage as figurative use).

V.iv PHILASTER

CAPTAIN.
No, you shall spare his dowcets, my dear donsels. As you respect the ladies, let them flourish. The curses of a longing woman kills as speedy as a plague, boys. 55

1 CITIZEN.
I'll have a leg, that's certain.

2 CITIZEN.
I'll have an arm.

3 CITIZEN.
I'll have his nose, and at mine own charge build a college and clap't upon the gate. 60

4 CITIZEN.
I'll have his little gut to string a kit with, for certainly a royal gut will sound like silver.

PHARAMOND.
Would they were in thy belly, and I past my pain once.

5 CITIZEN.
Good Captain, let me have his liver to feed ferrets. 65

CAPTAIN.
Who will have parcels else? Speak.

PHARAMOND.
Good gods, consider me! I shall be tortur'd.

1 CITIZEN.
Captain, I'll give you the trimming of your two-hand sword and let me have his skin to make false scabbards.

2 CITIZEN.
He had no horns, sir, had he? 70

---

55. *dowcets*] testes (as at IV.ii.13).
55. *donsels*] "i.e. youths . . . properly, young gentlemen professing arms and not yet knighted," derived from the name of the hero of a Spanish romance, Donzel del Phebo (Dyce). His exploits were translated into English in various parts from 1583 to 1601 under the title *The Mirror of Knighthood* (Daniel).
60–61. *nose . . . college*] a reference to Brasenose College, Oxford, chartered in 1512; "over the College gate was (and is) a grotesque brass face with a large nose" (Daniel Seltzer, ed., *Friar Bacon and Friar Bungay* [Lincoln, Nebr., 1963], p. 11 n.). Weber notes this passage as "a somewhat unappropriate allusion to Brazen-Nose College at Oxford."
62. *kit*] "a small violin" (Weber).
66. *parcels*] portions, parts.

CAPTAIN.
> No, sir, he's a pollard. What wouldst thou do with horns?

2 CITIZEN.
> Oh, if he had had, I would have made rare hafts and whistles of 'em; but his shin bones, if they be sound, shall serve me. 75

Enter Philaster.

ALL.
> Long live Philaster, the brave prince Philaster!

PHILASTER.
> I thank you, gentlemen. But why are these
> Rude weapons brought abroad, to teach your hands
> Uncivil trades?

CAPTAIN. My royal Rosicleer,
> We are thy myrmidons, thy guard, thy roarers, 80
> And when thy noble body is in durance,
> Thus do we clap our musty murrions on
> And trace the streets in terror. Is it peace,
> Thou Mars of men? Is the king sociable
> And bids thee live? Art thou above thy foeman 85
> And free as Phoebus? Speak. If not, this stand
> Of royal blood shall be abroach, a-tilt, and run

---

71. *pollard*] "unhorned beast" (Daniel).

73. *hafts*] handles, hilts.

79. *Rosicleer*] brother of Donzel del Phebo in *The Mirror of Knighthood* (Dyce).

80. *roarers*] "Or roaring boys, was a cant name for a set of quarrelsome bullying blades, who, when this play was written and long after, infested the streets of London" (Dyce). See earlier use of *myrmidons* at V.iv.1.

81. *durance*] imprisonment, forced confinement *(OED)*.

82. *murrions*] obsolete form of "morion," a helmet used by soldiers in the sixteenth and seventeenth centuries *(OED)*.

83. *trace*] pass along or over, tread, traverse *(OED)*.

86. *Phoebus*] another allusion to the Spanish romance *Donzel del Phebo* (Dyce).

87. *abroach*] astir; literally, as a cask is broached or pierced to draw out liquor *(OED)*. *A-tilt* in the present passage also suggests the

V.iv   PHILASTER

Even to the lees of honor.
PHILASTER.
Hold and be satisfied. I am myself,
Free as my thoughts are. By the gods, I am! 90
CAPTAIN.
Art thou the dainty darling of the king?
Art thou the Hylas to our Hercules?
Do the lords bow, and the regarded scarlets
Kiss their gumm'd golls and cry, "We are your servants"?
Is the court navigable and the presence stuck 95
With flags of friendship? If not, we are thy castle
And this man sleeps.
PHILASTER.
I am what I do desire to be, your friend.
I am what I was born to be, your prince.
PHARAMOND.
Sir, there is some humanity in you. 100
You have a noble soul. Forget my name
And know my misery. Set me safe aboard
From these wild cannibals, and as I live
I'll quit this land forever. There is nothing:
Perpetual prisonment, cold, hunger, sickness 105
Of all sorts, of all dangers, and altogether
The worst company of the worst men, madness, age,

---

drawing off of liquid. *Stand* (l. 86) can mean "tub" or "barrel" *(OED)*, here referring to Pharamond as a cask of royal blood ready to be drained.

88. *lees*] dregs.

92. *Hylas*] Hylas was the young armor-bearer to Hercules, referred to earlier at II.iv.17.

93-94. *the regarded . . . golls*] *Golls* are hands; *gumm'd* may mean "corrupted" (Daniel) or "anointed with gum for perfuming or bleaching" (Dyce). Daniel notes, "The *regarded scarlets* must, I think, refer to the judges or officers of state who have been bribed to put Philaster down, but who now kiss their corrupted hands and profess themselves his servants. Whether *regarded* should be taken in the sense of respected or *re-garded*, i.e. *re-laced*, I cannot determine."

95. *presence*] assemblage of people; a company present *(OED)*; the analogy concerns the court as a ship displaying flags denoting friendly intentions.

96. *castle*] fortress, bulwark.

—108—

PHILASTER V.iv

To be as many creatures as a woman
And do as they all do, nay, to despair;
But I would rather make it a new nature 110
And live with all these, than endure one hour
Amongst these wild dogs.

PHILASTER.
I do pity you. Friends, discharge your fears.
Deliver me the prince. I'll warrant you
I shall be old enough to find my safety. 115

3 CITIZEN.
Good sir, take heed he does not hurt you.
He's a fierce man, I can tell you, sir.

CAPTAIN.
Prince, by your leave, I'll have a surcingle
And make you like a hawk. *He strives.*

PHILASTER.
Away, away, there is no danger in him. 120
Alas, he had rather sleep to shake his fit off.
Look you, friends, how gently he leads. Upon my word,
He's tame enough; he needs no further watching.
Good my friends, go to your houses,
And by me have your pardons and my love, 125
And know there shall be nothing in my power
You may deserve but you shall have your wishes.
To give you more thanks were to flatter you.

---

110. *make it*] accept it (the unfavorable situation just described) as.
115. *old*] practiced, experienced; in slang use, clever, knowing *(OED)*.
118. *surcingle*] a girth or band, here one used in taming hawks.
119. *make*] a term in falconry meaning to order, fashion, render obedient (Dyce); to train, as a hawk *(OED)*. Most editors except Turner have adopted the Q8 and F reading *mail (male)*, meaning to bind a hawk's wings with a cloth *(OED* cites this passage in defining "mail").
119. S.D. *He strives*] i.e., Pharamond struggles; omitted by Dyce, Daniel.
123. *watching*] being awake; wakefulness. Mason notes that "one of the means used to tame hawks is to keep them continually awake" (quoted by Dyce).

V.iv   PHILASTER

    Continue still your love, and for an earnest
    Drink this.   [*Gives money.*]   130
ALL.
    Long mayst thou live, brave prince, brave prince, brave
    prince!   *Exeunt* Philaster *and* Pharamond.
CAPTAIN.
    Go thy ways, thou art the king of courtesy. Fall off
    again, my sweet youths. Come, and every man trace to
    his house again and hang his pewter up; then to the   135
    tavern, and bring your wives in muffs. We will have
    music, and the red grape shall make us dance and rise,
    boys.   *Exeunt.*

[V.v]   *Enter* King, Arethusa, *Galatea*, Megra, Cleremont,
               Dion, *Thrasiline*, Bellario, *and attendants.*

KING.
    Is it appeas'd?
DION.
    Sir, all is quiet as this dead of night,
    As peaceable as sleep. My lord Philaster
    Brings on the prince himself.
KING.   Kind gentlemen,
    I will not break the least word I have given   5
    In promise to him. I have heap'd a world
    Of grief upon his head, which yet I hope
    To wash away.

               Enter Philaster *and* Pharamond.

CLEREMONT.   My lord is come.
KING.   My son,
    Blest be the time that I have leave to call

---

    129. *earnest*] pledge, token. Dyce adds the stage direction at l. 130, "*Gives money*"; Q1 reads, "*Gives 'em his purse.*"
    135. *pewter*] alloy of tin and lead, here meaning armor *(OED,* citing this passage and the term "pewter coat" or coat of mail).
    136. *muffs*] warm covering for the hands.
[V.v]
    1. *appeas'd*] pacified, calmed.

Such virtue mine. Now thou art in mine arms, 10
Methinks I have a salve unto my breast
For all the stings that dwell there. Streams of grief
That I have wrought thee, and as much of joy
That I repent it, issue from mine eyes.
Let them appease thee. Take thy right. Take her; 15
She is thy right, too, and forget to urge
My vexed soul with that I did before.

PHILASTER.
Sir, it is blotted from my memory,
Past and forgotten. For you, prince of Spain,
Whom I have thus redeem'd, you have full leave 20
To make an honorable voyage home.
And if you would go furnish'd to your realm
With fair provision, I do see a lady
Methinks would gladly bear you company.
How like you this piece?

MEGRA. Sir, he likes it well, 25
For he hath tried it and hath found it worth
His princely liking. We were ta'en abed.
I know your meaning. I am not the first
That nature taught to seek a fellow forth.
Can shame remain perpetually in me 30
And not in others? Or have princes salves
To cure ill names that meaner people want?

PHILASTER.
What mean you?

MEGRA. You must get another ship
To bear the princess and her boy together.

DION.
How now? 35

MEGRA.
Others took me, and I took her and him

---

13. *wrought*] emended to "wrong'd" by Theobald, followed by most later editors. *Wrought* stands in Q2–9 and F (no corresponding passage in Q1) and may be meant in the obsolete sense of "agitated"; or it could refer to the grief that the king has wrought (created) for Pharamond.

32. *want*] lack.

V.v   PHILASTER

> At that all women may be ta'en sometime.
> Ship us all four, my lord. We can endure
> Weather and wind alike.

KING.
> Clear thou thyself, or know not me for father.   40

ARETHUSA.
> This earth, how false it is. What means is left for me
> To clear myself? It lies in your belief.
> My lords, believe me, and let all things else
> Struggle together to dishonor me.

BELLARIO.
> Oh, stop your ears, great king, that I may speak   45
> As freedom would. Then I will call this lady
> As base as are her actions. Hear me, sir.
> Believe your heated blood when it rebels
> Against your reason sooner than this lady.

MEGRA.
> By this good light, he bears it handsomely.   50

PHILASTER.
> This lady! I will sooner trust the wind
> With feathers, or the troubl'd sea with pearl,
> Than her with anything. Believe her not!
> Why, think you if I did believe her words
> I would outlive 'em? Honor cannot take   55
> Revenge on you. Then what were to be known
> But death?

KING.   Forget her, sir, since all is knit
> Between us. But I must request of you
> One favor and will sadly be denied.

PHILASTER.
> Command, whate'er it be.   60

KING.
> Swear to be true to what you promise.

PHILASTER.
> By the powers above,
> Let it not be the death of her or him,
> And it is granted.

---

59. *will . . . denied*] "i.e. shall be very sorry to be denied" (Theobald). Daniel suggests "hardly" for *sadly*.

—112—

KING.   Bear away that boy
To torture. I will have her clear'd or buried.

PHILASTER.
Oh, let me call my word back, worthy sir!
Ask something else. Bury my life and right
In one poor grave, but do not take away
My life and fame at once.

KING.
Away with him! It stands irrevocable.

PHILASTER.
Turn all your eyes on me. Here stands a man
The falsest and the basest of this world.
Set swords against this breast, some honest man,
For I have liv'd till I am pitied.
My former deeds were hateful, but this last
Is pitiful, for I unwillingly
Have given the dear preserver of my life
Unto his torture. Is it in the power
Of flesh and blood to carry this and live?
            Offers to kill himself.

ARETHUSA.
Dear sir, be patient yet. Oh, stay that hand!

KING.
Sirs, strip that boy.

DION.
Come, sir, your tender flesh will try your constancy.

BELLARIO.
Oh, kill me, gentlemen!

DION.
No. Help, sirs.

BELLARIO.
Will you torture me?

KING.
Haste there. Why stay you?

BELLARIO.
Then I shall not break my vow,
You know, just gods, though I discover all.

KING.
How's that? Will he confess?

V.v   Philaster

DION.
    Sir, so he says.   90
KING.
    Speak, then.
BELLARIO.
    Great king, if you command
    This lord to talk with me alone, my tongue,
    Urg'd by my heart, shall utter all the thoughts
    My youth hath known; and stranger things than these   95
    You hear not often.
KING.
    Walk aside with him.

        [Dion *and* Bellario *walk apart.*]

DION.
    Why speak'st thou not?
BELLARIO.
    Know you this face, my lord?
DION.
    No.   100
BELLARIO.
    Have you not seen it, nor the like?
DION.
    Yes, I have seen the like, but readily
    I know not where.
BELLARIO.   I have been often told
    In court of one Euphrasia, a lady
    And daughter to you; betwixt whom and me   105
    They that would flatter my bad face would swear
    There was such strange resemblance that we two
    Could not be known asunder, dress'd alike.
DION.
    By heaven, and so there is!
BELLARIO.   For her fair sake
    Who now doth spend the springtime of her life   110
    In holy pilgrimage, move to the king
    That I may 'scape this torture.

97.1.] added by Dyce.

PHILASTER V.v

DION. But thou speak'st
As like Euphrasia as thou dost look.
How came it to thy knowledge that she lives
In pilgrimage?
BELLARIO. I know it not, my lord, 115
But I have heard it and do scarce believe it.
DION.
Oh, my shame, is't possible? Draw near
That I may gaze upon thee. Art thou she,
Or else her murderer? Where wert thou born?
BELLARIO.
In Syracusa.
DION. What's thy name?
BELLARIO. Euphrasia. 120
DION.
Oh, 'tis just; 'tis she!
Now I do know thee. Oh, that thou hadst died
And I had never seen thee, nor my shame.
How shall I own thee? Shall this tongue of mine
E'er call thee daughter more? 125
BELLARIO.
Would I had died indeed! I wish it, too;
And so must have done by vow ere publish'd
What I have told, but that there was no means
To hide it longer. Yet I joy in this:
The princess is all clear.
KING. What, have you done? 130
DION.
All's discover'd.

---

119. *her murderer*] "It was the received opinion in some barbarous countries, that the murderer was to inherit the qualities and shape of the person he destroyed" (Mason, quoted by Weber).

120. *Euphrasia*] Q1, Turner give the stage direction *"Kneels to Dion [Q1 Leon], and discovers her hair."* This staging is appropriate for Q1, where the private conversation between father and daughter is omitted, but does not seem feasible here because other characters on stage await Dion's announcement of Bellario's identity (l. 134 below).

127. *by vow*] explained in a subsequent speech (see l. 186 below).

—115—

V.v   PHILASTER

PHILASTER.   Why, then, hold you me?
All is discover'd. Pray you, let me go.
                    He offers to stab himself.
KING.
     Stay him.
ARETHUSA.   What is discover'd?
DION.   Why, my shame.
     It is a woman. Let her speak the rest.
PHILASTER.
     How? That again!
DION.   It is a woman.   135
PHILASTER.
     Blest be you powers that favor innocence!
KING.
     Lay hold upon that lady.   [Megra *is seized.*]
PHILASTER.
     It is a woman, sir! Hark, gentlemen,
     It is a woman! Arethusa, take
     My soul into thy breast, that would be gone   140
     With joy. It is a woman! Thou art fair
     And virtuous still to ages, in despite of malice.
KING.
     Speak you, where lies his shame?
BELLARIO.
     I am his daughter.
PHILASTER.
     The gods are just.   145
DION.
     I dare accuse none, but before you two,
     The virtue of our age, I bend my knee
     For mercy.
PHILASTER.   Take it freely, for I know
     Though what thou didst were undiscreetly done,
     'Twas meant well.
ARETHUSA.   And for me,   150
     I have a power to pardon sins as oft
     As any man has power to wrong me.
CLEREMONT.
     Noble and worthy.

PHILASTER.   But Bellario
(For I must call thee still so), tell me why
Thou didst conceal thy sex. It was a fault, 155
A fault, Bellario, though thy other deeds
Of truth outweigh'd it. All these jealousies
Had flown to nothing if thou hadst discover'd
What now we know.
BELLARIO.   My father oft would speak
Your worth and virtue, and as I did grow 160
More and more apprehensive, I did thirst
To see the man so rais'd. But yet all this
Was but a maiden-longing, to be lost
As soon as found; till sitting in my window
Printing my thoughts in lawn, I saw a god, 165
I thought, but it was you, enter our gates.
My blood flew out and back again, as fast
As I had puff'd it forth and suck'd it in
Like breath. Then was I call'd away in haste
To entertain you. Never was a man 170
Heav'd from a sheepcote to a scepter, rais'd
So high in thoughts as I. You left a kiss
Upon these lips then, which I mean to keep
From you forever. I did hear you talk,
Far above singing. After you were gone, 175
I grew acquainted with my heart and search'd
What stirr'd it so. Alas, I found it love,
Yet far from lust; for could I but have liv'd
In presence of you, I had had my end.
For this I did delude my noble father 180
With a feign'd pilgrimage and dress'd myself
In habit of a boy. And for I knew

---

161. *apprehensive*] discerning, capable of apprehending.

162. *rais'd*] emended by Theobald, Dyce, other editors to *prais'd*; Q2–9 and F read *rais'd*.

165. *Printing . . . lawn*] embroidering designs on soft cotton or linen fabric. *Print* is used in the sense of impress or fix on a surface or object.

182. *for*] because.

V.v   PHILASTER

    My birth no match for you, I was past hope
    Of having you. And understanding well
    That when I made discovery of my sex   185
    I could not stay with you, I made a vow
    By all the most religious things a maid
    Could call together, never to be known
    Whilst there was hope to hide me from men's eyes
    For other than I seem'd, that I might ever   190
    Abide with you. Then sat I by the fount
    Where first you took me up.
KING.   Search out a match
    Within our kingdom, where and when thou wilt,
    And I will pay thy dowry, and thyself
    Wilt well deserve him.
BELLARIO.   Never, sir, will I   195
    Marry. It is a thing within my vow.
    But if I may have leave to serve the princess,
    To see the virtues of her lord and her,
    I shall have hope to live.
ARETHUSA.   I, Philaster,
    Cannot be jealous, though you had a lady   200
    Dress'd like a page to serve you, nor will I
    Suspect her living here. Come, live with me;
    Live free as I do. She that loves my lord,
    Curst be the wife that hates her.
PHILASTER.
    I grieve such virtue should be laid in earth   205
    Without an heir. Hear me, my royal father.
    Wrong not the freedom of our souls so much
    To think to take revenge of that base woman.
    Her malice cannot hurt us. Set her free
    As she was born, saving from shame and sin.   210
KING.
    Set her at liberty. But leave the court;
    There is no place for such. You, Pharamond,
    Shall have free passage, and a conduct home
    Worthy so great a prince. When you come there,
    Remember 'twas your faults that lost you her   215
    And not my purpos'd will.

PHARAMOND.
I do confess, renowned sir.
KING.
Last, join your hands in one. Enjoy, Philaster,
This kingdom, which is yours, and after me
Whatever I call mine. My blessing on you. 220
All happy hours be at your marriage joys,
That you may grow yourselves over all lands
And live to see your plenteous branches spring
Wherever there is sun. Let princes learn
By this to rule the passions of their blood, 225
For what heaven wills can never be withstood.

Exeunt omnes.

FINIS

---

221. *happy hours*] probably "fortunate times," although there may be a reference to the Hours or female divinities presiding over the changing seasons; these are referred to in Thomas Gray's *Odes, Spring*, i, as "fair Venus' train" *(OED)*.

Appendix A

The Beginning and Ending of the Q1 Text

The first 87 lines of the 1620 quarto (B1 recto and verso, B2 recto) and the last 205 lines (I2 verso, from twelfth line on; I3 recto and verso; I4 recto and verso; K recto and verso) are given here. Spelling and punctuation are modernized, but the predominating Q1 spelling is retained in the characters' names: Lyon (Leon) for Dion, Clerimon for Cleremont, Trasiline for Thrasaline, Pharamont for Pharamond, Phylaster for Philaster. A brief account of the textual differences between Q1 and Q2 may be found in the Introduction.

PHYLASTER

[I.i]
Enter at several doors Lord Lyon, Trasiline *follows him,* Clerimon *meets them.*

TRASILINE.
  Well o'er ta'en, my lord.
LYON.
  Noble friend, welcome; and see who encounters us—
  honorable, good Clerimon.
CLERIMON.
  My good lord Lyon; most happily met, worthy Trasiline.
  Come, gallants, what's the news? The season affords us   5
  variety; the novelists of our time run on heaps to glut

---

6. *novelists*] innovators; introducers or favorers of something new (*OED*).

—121—

The Q1 Text

their itching ears with airy sounds, trotting to the burse, and in the temple walk with greater zeal to hear a novel lie than a pious anthem, though chanted by cherubims.

TRASILINE.

True, sir, and hold set councils to vent their brainsick opinions with presagements what all states shall design.

CLERIMON.

That's as their intelligence serves.

LYON.

And that shall serve as long as invention lasts. Their dreams they relate as spoke from oracles; or if the gods should hold a synod and make them their secretaries, they will divine and prophesy, too. But come and speak your thoughts of the intended marriage with the Spanish prince. He is come, you see, and bravely entertain'd.

TRASILINE.

He is so, but not married yet.

CLERIMON.

But like to be, and shall have in dowry with the princess this kingdom of Sicily.

LEON.

Soft and fair, there is more will forbid the bans than say "amen" to the marriage. Though the king usurp'd the kingdom during the nonage of the prince Phylaster, he must not think to bereave him of it quite. He is now come to years to claim the crown.

TRASILINE.

And lose his head i'the asking.

LEON.

A diadem worn by a headless king would be wondrous. Phylaster is too weak in power.

CLERIMON.

He hath many friends.

---

7. *burse*] meeting place for merchants for business transactions; an exchange, either the New Exchange in the Strand (1609) or the Royal Exchange (1566) *(OED)*.

Appendix A

LEON.
　And few helpers.
TRASILINE.
　The people love him.
LEON.
　I grant it; that, the king knows too well
　And makes this contract to make his faction strong.　35
　What's a giddy-headed multitude
　That's not disciplin'd nor train'd up in arms
　To be trusted unto? No, he that will
　Bandy for a monarchy must provide
　Brave martial troops with resolution arm'd　40
　To stand the shock of bloody, doubtful war;
　Not daunted though disastrous fate doth frown
　And spit all spiteful fury in their face,
　Defying horror in her ugliest form,
　And grows more valiant, the more danger threats.　45
　Or let lean famine her affliction send,
　Whose pining plagues a second hell doth bring,
　They'll hold their courage in her height of spleen
　Till valor win plenty to supply them.
　What think you, would your feast-hunting citizens　50
　Endure this?
TRASILINE.
　No, sir, a fair march a mile out of town
　That their wives may bring them their dinners,
　Is the hottest service that they are train'd up to.
CLERIMON.
　I could wish their experience answer'd their loves.　55
　Then should the much-too-much wrong'd Phylaster
　Possess his right in spite of don and the devil.
TRASILINE.
　My heart is with your wishes.
LEON.　　　　　　　　　　And so is mine,
　And so should all that love their true-born prince.
　Then let us join our forces with our minds　60
　In what's our power to right this wronged lord,

---

57. *don*] Pharamont, the Spanish nobleman.

The Q1 Text

And watch advantage as best may fit the time
To stir the murmuring people up;
Who is already possess'd with his wrongs
And easily would in rebellion rise, 65
Which full well the king doth both know and fear.
But first our service we'll proffer to the prince
And set our projects as he accepts of us.
But hush, the king is coming. *Sound music within.*

Enter the King, Pharamont, *the Princess, the Lady* Gallatea, *the Lady* Megra, *a Gentlewoman, with Lords attending; the* King *takes his seat.*

KING.   Fair prince,
Since heaven's great guider furthers our intents 70
And brought you with safety here to arrive
Within our kingdom and court of Sicily,
We bid you most welcome, princely Pharamont,
And that our kingly bounty shall confirm;
Even whilst the heavens hold so propitious aspect, 75
We'll crown your wish'd desires with our own.
Lend me your hand, sweet prince. Hereby enjoy
A full fruition of your best contents.
The interest I hold I do possess you with,
Only a father's care and prayers retain 80
That heaven may heap on blessings. Take her, prince,
A sweeter mistress than the offer'd language of any dame,

[V.iv]
Enter an old Captain, *with a crew of* Citizens, *leading* Pharamont *prisoner.*

CAPTAIN.

Come, my brave myrmidons, fall on! Let your caps swarm and your nimble tongues forget your gibberish of what-you-lack; and set your mouths ope, children, till your palates fall frighted half a fathom, past the cure of bay-salt and gross pepper, and then cry "Phylaster, 5
brave Phylaster!" Let Phylaster be deep in request, my ding-a-dings, my pair of dear indentures, king of clubs, than your cut-water-camlets and your painting. Let not

Appendix A

your hasty silks, dearly belovers of custards and cheese-
cakes, or your branch cloth of bodkins, or your tiffanies, 10
your Robin-Hood, Scarlet, and Johns, tie your affections
in durance to your shops, my dainty duckers. Up with
your three-pil'd spirits, that right valorous, and let your
acute colors make the king to feel the measure of your
mightiness. Phylaster! Cry, my rose-nobles, cry! 15

OMNES.

Phylaster, Phylaster!

CAPTAIN.

How do you like this, my lord prisoner? These are mad
boys, I can tell you; these be things that will not strike
top-sail to a foist and let a man-of-war, an argosy, stoop
to carry coals. 20

PHARAMONT.

Why, you damn'd slaves, do you know who I am?

CAPTAIN.

Yes, my pretty prince of puppets, we do know, and give
you gentle warning: you talk no more such bug words,
lest that sodden crown should be scratch'd with a musket.
Dear prince pippin, I'll have you coddled. Let him loose, 25
my spirits, and make a ring with your bills, my hearts.
Now let me see what this brave man dares do. Note, sir,
have at you with this washing blow; here I lie. Do you
huff, sweet prince? I could hock your grace and hang
you cross-legg'd, like a hare at a poulter's stall, and do 30
thus.

PHARAMONT.

Gentlemen, honest gentlemen—

1 SOLDIER.

He speaks treason, captain. Shall's knock him down?

CAPTAIN.

Hold, I say.

2 SOLDIER.

Good captain, let me have one mall at's mazard. I feel 35

---

10. *tiffanies*] very thin silk; gauze.
35. *mall*] or maul, a heavy blow with a hammer or club *(OED)*.
35. *mazard*] jocular archaism for the head *(OED)*.

The Q1 Text

my stomach strangely provoked to be at his Spanish pot-noll. Shall's kill him?

OMNES.

Ay, kill him, kill him!

CAPTAIN.

Again I say hold.

3 SOLDIER.

Oh how rank he looks, sweet captain! Let's geld him and send his dowcets for a dish to the bordello.

4 SOLDIER.

No, let's rather sell them to some woman chemist, that extractions, she might draw an excellent provocative oil from useth them, that might be very useful.

CAPTAIN.

You see, my scurvy don, how precious you are in esteem amongst us. Had you not been better kept at home? I think you had. Must you needs come amongst us, to have your saffron hide taw'd as we intend it? My don, Phylaster must suffer death to satisfy your melancholy spleen. He must, my don, he must! But we, your physicians, hold it fit that you bleed for it. Come, my robustics, my brave regiment of rattle makers, let's call a common cornuted council, and like grave senators bear up our branch'd crests in sitting upon the several tortures we shall put him to, and with as little sense as may be, put your wills in execution.

SOME CRYS.

Burn him, burn him!

OTHERS.

Hang him, hang him!

---

37. *pot-noll*] *Noll* means head; *pot* may signify the skull or brainpan but probably here refers to a steel cap or small helmet, worn especially by the cavalry in the seventeenth century *(OED)*.

41. *bordello*] brothel.

44. *useth*] Daniel (p. 127) notes that "useth (-useth to make) is evidently out of its place; it should come before *extractions* in the preceding line."

53. *cornuted*] literally, "horned," i.e., cuckolded.

Appendix A

Enter Phylaster.

CAPTAIN.
No, rather let's carbonate his cods-head and cut him to collops. Shall I begin? 60

PHYLASTER.
Stay your furies, my loving countrymen.

OMNES.
Phylaster is come! Phylaster, Phylaster!

CAPTAIN.
My porcupines of spite, make room, I say, that I may salute my brave prince; and is Prince Phylaster at liberty?

PHYLASTER.
I am, most loving countrymen. 65

CAPTAIN.
Then give me thy princely goll, which thus I kiss, to whom I crouch and bow. But see, my royal spark, this headstrong swarm that follow me humming like a master bee, have I led forth their hives; and being on wing, and in our heady flight, have seized him shall suffer for 70 thy wrongs.

OMNES.
Ay, ay, let's kill him! Kill him!

PHYLASTER.
But hear me, countrymen.

CAPTAIN.
Hear the prince, I say, hear Phylaster.

OMNES.
Ay, ay, hear the prince, hear the prince! 75

PHYLASTER.
My coming is to give you thanks, my dear countrymen, whose powerful sway hath curb'd the prosecuting fury of my foes.

OMNES.
We will curb 'em, we will curb 'em!

---

59. *carbonate his cods-head*] burn his stupid head.
60. *collops*] small portions of food, usually meat.
66. *goll*] hand

—127—

The Q1 Text

PHYLASTER.

I find you will; but if my interest in your loves be such 80
as the world takes notice of, let me crave you would
deliver Pharamont to my hand and from me accept this
testimony of my love *(gives 'em his purse),* which is but
a pittance of those ample thanks which shall redound
with shower'd courtesies. 85

CAPTAIN.

Take him to thee, brave prince, and we thy bounty
thankfully accept and will drink thy health, thy perpetual health, my prince, whilst memory lasts amongst
us. We are thy myrmidons, my Achilles; we are those
will follow thee and in thy service will scour our rusty 90
murrins and our bill-bow-blades; most notable Phylaster,
we will! Come, my rowtists, let's retire till occasion
calls us to attend the noble Phylaster.

OMNES.

Phylaster, Phylaster, Phylaster!

Exit Captain *and citizens.*

PHARAMONT.

Worthy sir, I owe you a life; for but yourself, there's 95
naught could have prevail'd.

PHYLASTER.

'Tis the least of service that I owe the king, who was
careful to preserve you. *Exeunt.*

[V.v]   *Enter* Leon, Trasiline, *and* Clerimon.

TRASILINE.

I ever thought the boy was honest.

LEON.

Well, 'tis a brave boy, gentlemen.

CLERIMON.

Yet you'd not believe this.

---

91. *murrins*] or morions, a soldier's helmet lacking a beaver or visor *(OED).*

91. *bill-bow-blades*] swords from Bilbao, Spain, noted for the strength and elasticity of the blades *(OED).*

92. *rowtists*] from "rowty," meaning coarse, rough, rank *(OED);* "rowdy" seems to be a later and probably unrelated word.

Appendix A

LEON.
> A plague on my forwardness! What a villain was I, to wrong 'em so! A mischief on my muddy brains, was I mad?

TRASILINE.
> A little frantic in your rash attempt, but that was your love to Phylaster, sir.

LEON.
> A pox on such love! Have you any hope my countenance will e'er serve me to look on them?

CLERIMON.
> Oh, very well, sir.

LEON.
> Very ill, sir! 'Uds death, I could beat out my brains, or hang myself in revenge!

CLERIMON.
> There would be little gotten by it; e'en keep you as you are.

LEON.
> An excellent boy, gentlemen, believe it. Hark, the king is coming.   *Cornets sound.*

Enter the King, Princess, Gallatea, Megra, Bellario, *a Gentlewoman, and other attendants.*

KING.
> No news of his return.
> Will not this rabble multitude be appeas'd?
> I fear their outrage, lest it should extend
> With dangering of Pharamont's life.

Enter Phylaster *with* Pharamont.

LEON.
> See, sir, Phylaster is return'd.

PHYLASTER.   Royal sir.
> Receive into your bosom your desired peace.

---

12. *'Uds*] God's (in oaths).
13. *revenge*] punishment, chastisement; also in the sense of avenging, as a person *(OED)*.

The Q1 Text

  Those discontented mutineers be appeas'd
  And this foreign prince in safety.   25
KING.
  How happy am I in thee, Phylaster,
  Whose excellent virtues beget a world of love!
  I am indebted to thee for a kingdom.
  I here surrender up all sovereignty;
  Reign peacefully with thy espoused bride.   30
  Assume, my son, to take what is thy due.
          Delivers his crown to him.
PHARAMONT.
  How, sir, your son? What am I, then?
  Your daughter you gave to me.
KING.
  But heaven hath made assignment unto him
  And brought your contract to annullity.   35
  Sir, your entertainment hath been most fair,
  Had not your hell-bred lust dried up the spring
  From whence flow'd forth those favors that you found.
  I am glad to see you safe; let this suffice.
  Yourself hath cross'd yourself.
LEON.   They are married, sir.   40
PHARAMONT.
  How, married! I hope your highness will not use me so.
  I came not to be disgrac'd and return alone.
KING.
  I cannot help it, sir.
LEON.
  To return alone, you need not, sir.
  Here is one will bear you company.   45
  You know this lady's proof, if you
  Fail'd not in the say-taking.
MEGRA.
  I hold your scoffs in vilest base contempt;
  Or is there said or done aught I repent,
  But can retort even to your grinning teeths,   50

---

47. *say-taking*] assay-taking, testing by trial; Q1 reads "say-taging," presumably a misprint.

—130—

Appendix A

    Your worst of spites. Though princess' lofty steps
    May not be trac'd, yet may they tread awry.
    That boy there—
BELLARIO.   If to me ye speak, lady,
    I must tell you, you have lost yourself
    In your too much forwardness and hath forgot   55
    Both modesty and truth. With what impudence
    You have thrown most damnable aspersions
    On that noble princess and myself, witness the world!
    Behold me, sir.   *Kneels to* Leon *and discovers her hair.*
LEON.
    I should know this face. My daughter!
BELLARIO.   The same, sir.   60
PRINCESS.
    How, our sometime page Bellario turn'd woman?
BELLARIO.
    Madam, the cause induc'd me to transform myself
    Proceeded from a respective modest
    Affection I bore to my lord,
    The prince Phylaster, to do him service,   65
    As far from any lascivious thought
    As that lady is far from goodness.
    And if my true intents may be believ'd
    And from your highness, madam, pardon find,
    You have the truth.   70
PRINCESS.
    I do believe thee; "Bellario" I shall call thee still.
PHYLASTER.
    The faithfullest servant that ever gave attendance!
LEON.
    Now, lady lust, what say you to the boy now?
    Do you hang the head, do you? Shame would steal
    Into your face if you had grace to entertain it.   75
    Do you slink away?   *Exit* Megra *hiding her face.*
KING.
    Give present order she be banish'd the court
    And straightly confin'd till our further

---

78. *straightly*] the Q1 spelling; the meaning may be "straitly" (strictly, narrowly).

The Q1 Text

Pleasure is known.

PHARAMONT.
    Here's such an age of transformation that I do not know 80
how to trust myself. I'll get me gone, too. Sir, the disparagement you have done must be call'd in question.
I have power to right myself, and will.   *Exit* Pharamont.

KING.
    We fear you not, sir.

PHYLASTER.
    Let a strong convoy guard him through the kingdom. 85
With him, let's part with all our cares and fear,
And crown with joy our happy love's success.

KING.
    Which to make more full, Lady Gallatea,
Let honor'd Clerimon acceptance find
In your chaste thoughts.

PHYLASTER.   'Tis my suit, too. 90

PRINCESS.
    Such royal spokesmen must not be denied.

GALLATEA.
    Nor shall not, madam.

KING.   Then thus I join your hands.

GALLATEA.
    Our hearts were knit before.   *They kiss.*

PHYLASTER [*to* Bellario].
    But 'tis you, lady, must make all complete,
And give a full period to content. 95
Let your love's cordial again revive
The drooping spirits of noble Trasiline.
What says lord Leon to it?

LEON.
    Marry, my lord, I say I know she once lov'd him,
At least made show she did. 100
But since 'tis my lord Phylaster's desire,
I'll make a surrender of all the right
A father has in her. Here, take her, sir,
With all my heart, and heaven give you joy.

---

96. *cordial*] a stimulant, especially a medicine for the heart.

Appendix A

KING.
>Then let us in these nuptial feasts to hold, 105
>Heaven hath decreed and fate stands uncontrol'd.

FINIS

Appendix B

Principal Substantive Variants in Early Texts

Listed here, with spelling and punctuation modernized, is a selection of the principal substantive variants among the texts of the nine early quartos of *Philaster* and the Second Folio. The present edition follows Q2 except where noted. Because of the unusual number of variant readings found in Q1, only the more significant ones are listed; and because variants in Q3-9 and F are reprint errors, only a representative sample of these is presented. Omitted are changes in tense of verbs and number of nouns and pronouns; shifts in word order; repetition and inconsequential addition of words and phrases; most euphemized oaths; variations in speech prefixes (usually Q1 errors); variant spellings; and "accidentals" such as punctuation and verse lineation. The widely variant beginning and concluding portions of Q1 are given in Appendix A and hence omitted here except for a few readings early in V.iv. A complete historical collation of early texts may be found in the Cambridge edition of Beaumont and Fletcher (Vol. I, ed. Robert K. Turner [1966]).

[I.i]
0.1–106] *See Appendix A for Q1 version.*
84. stronger] stranger Q-4–8, F.
88. our] your Q6–8, F.
89. our] your Q3, 5–6, 9; you Q4.
103. talk of] speak Q3–9, F; speaks Q5.
112. a] Q1; *om.* Q2.
139. eating] rotting Q1.
140. Open] Opine F; *see ex. n.*
157. Miraculous] Miracles Q1.
161. prais'd] be prais'd Q1.
162. speeches] praises Q1.
165. one sinew] unseen to Q1.
170. your] for Q1.
171. He fears] with fear Q4–8, F.
173. 'em] on Q1.
179. stare] start Q1.
181. fair] sweet Q1.
196. her] his Q1.
197. the just gods] Nemesis Q4–8, F.
200. popinjays] popines Q1.
206. call our physicians] choler Q1.
210. gentlemen. By heaven] gentle heavens Q1; gentlemen, by these hilts Q4–8, F.
227. belied] bellied Q3–9, F; *see ex. n.*
228. spite . . . bugs] Q3–F; spit all those brags Q1; Spite of these bugs Q2.

Principal Substantive Variants

230–231. to brave . . . frown] *om.* Q1.
235. He] this Q1.
238. th'other is] I'm sure t'other's Q1.
243. now nothing] now nought but Q4–8, F.
245. right me] right me not Q3–9, F.
250. not] *om.* Q1.
250. for all men] *om.* Q1.
251. through . . . faces] though men's faces Q1.
253. you] the Q1.
254. tenant] truant Q1; *see ex. n.*
256. have] am Q1.
260. brow] self o'er Q1.
265. man] Q1; men Q2.
268. It's] is Q1.
308. injuries] virtues Q1.
309. add] call Q1.
316. ears] years Q5–8, F.
336. do] dare Q1.
338. face] cheeks Q1.

[I.ii]
21. winning] wooing Q1.
26. her] his Q1.
28. contrary] bound to put Q1.
33. dooms] dens Q1.
41. beseem] become Q1.
50. fam'd] found Q1.
57. or I die] I do Q1.
58. may] die Q1.
70. can] cannot Q3–9, F.
77. lady's voice] woman's tongue Q1.
80. ask] beg Q1.
104. nobler] worthier Q1.
120. bay] vale Q1; *see ex. n.*
130. their courses] the course Q1.
131. light] life Q1.
149. God] Jove Q4–8, F.

150. hide me not] do not hide myself Q1.
159. For . . . do] *om.* Q1.
160.1.] *Q1 adds: and a woman.*
164. Writ in] Q3–9, F; within Q1; Writ it Q2.
165. no directlier] or no, directly Q1.
172. lie] be Q3–9, F.
175. thou] then Q1.
181. nought] nothing Q1.
198. hands] hearts Q1.
200. form] for me Q7–8, F.
202. such] your Q1.

[II.i]
0.1. and Bellario] *and his boy, called* Bellario Q1.
54. fights] sighs Q1.

[II.ii]
8. Madam] Q1 *only; see ex. n.*
19. coach] couch Q1.
20. a banquet] a play and a banquet Q1.
21. to blush . . . for] to make you blush Q1.
21–22. This . . . covers] this is my own hair Q1.
25. mercer's] silk-man's Q1.
26. good doings] doing Q1.
28.] *Q1 adds two speeches after this line; see ex. n.*
35. eight] five Q1.
38. spirits] animals Q1.
39. while] time Q1.
42. Danaë] dainty Q1.
43. in] with Q1.
49. gold] gold safe Q1.
52. I'll match ye] *om.* Q1.
52. S.D. *Exit . . . hangings*] *She slips behind the Arras* Q1 *(at l.49; here Q1 prints: Exit).*

—135—

Appendix B

65. talk] take Q2 *(in uncorrected copies; see Turner, p. 492)*, Q8, F.
68. or] your Q1.
69. theme] time Q1.
74. bright] deep Q1.
77. faint] sweet Q1.
78. and live] Q1 *adds: They kiss.*
81. nun] number Q1.
81. probation] Probatum Q1.
88. S.D. *Kisses her*] *They kiss* Q1; *om.* Q2-9, F.
89. I . . . before] you ha' done't before me Q1.
104. any . . . imaginations] my . . . imagination Q1.
109. any] my Q1.
110. Tim the] Timen a Q1.
110. leap] keep Q1.
119-120. Look . . . bolt] *om.* Q1.
128. Two hours] worship Q1.
132. unsafe] uncertain Q1.
137. Towsabell] Dowsabell Q1.

[II.iii]
17. she] they Q1; we Q7.
35. Thou disclaim'st] Then trust Q1.
40. curst master] cross schoolmaster Q1.
45. himself] itself Q1.
47. Love, madam] *om.* Q1.
53. think] sigh Q4-8, F.
54. Mingled with] with mingling Q1.
61. a bead] beads Q1; a beard Q2 *uncorr. (Turner, p. 492)*.
63-64. lie/ For] *om.* Q1.

[II.iv]
0.1.] *Enter the three Gentlewomen,* Megra, Gallatea, *and another Lady* Q1.
2. talk] take Q8, F.

6. thee'll] you'll Q1, 3-9, F.
7.1.] *Q1 adds: the princess' boy, and a woman.*
10. pleasant] pleasing Q1.
19. he] that Q1.
49. S.D. *Exit* Dion] Q1; *om.* Q2-9, F.
63. understanding] undeserving Q1.
66. by] in Q1.
77. get] get from them Q1.
82. Louder yet] *om.* Q1.
83. their . . . their] your . . . your Q1.
84. again] again, and louder Q1.
85-86. his/ Larum] such larums Q1.
86. prince] Q1 *adds S.D.: They knock.*
96. some] certain Q1.
96. myself] *Q1 adds S.D.: They press to come in.*
104. renegados] runagates Q1.
110. and ready] *om.* Q1.
120. yet] still Q1.
123. wring] wrong Q7-8, F; w rong Q6.
129. stage] Q1; stag Q2-9, F; *see ex. n.*
133. be not] *Q1 adds S.D.: they come down to the king.*
137. a 'pothecary] Apothecaries Q1.
158. lays . . . outlays] fair leaps And out-lying Q1.
169. fall] sink Q1.
170. a] in Q1.
182-183. Do . . . forget you] Do so, and I'll forget your —Q1.
185. Worthies] worthy Q1.
188. nettled] Q1; mettled Q2-3; melted Q9.
189. scarce] not Q1.

—136—

Principal Substantive Variants

[III.i]
1. Nay] And Q1.
7. down] Q1; drown Q2–3.
12. prince] thing Q1.
18. Philaster . . . himself] *om.* Q1.
25. confute] comfort Q1.
30. Upon his faith] on his belief Q1.
32. tends] Lords Q1.
41. frown] frame Q1.
49. or known] knows Q1; or knew Q3–9, F.
52. none] more Q1.
68. Thus] then Q1.
72. fruitful] faithful Q1.
74. off] out Q1.
74. whilst it springs] where it grows Q1.
92. womankind is false] Q2–3; women all are false Q1; that all woman-kind is false Q4–7; that all womenkind is false Q8, F.
97–98. for . . . possible] *om.* Q1.
105. coldly] milder Q1.
108. he] she Q1.
118. thunder on] daggers in Q1.
120. foul deed] fault Q1.
125. Kiss . . . one] Meets not a fair on Q1.
134. lodging forth] lodgings Q1.
136 S.P.–137. THRASILINE . . . mind] *om.* Q1.
138. them] her Q1.
141. fan] flame Q1.
143. This] the Q1.
157. blasted] blush Q1.
162. S.D. *Gives . . . letter*] *om.* Q2–9, F; *He gives him a letter* Q1.
167. Though] But Q1.
167. who] that Q1.
170. by] with Q1.
171. mines] twines Q1.
175. For . . . that] *om.* Q1.

185. loving secrets] maiden store Q1.
188. Regarded] rewarded Q1.
191. ill] well Q1.
193. not from off] out from Q1.
193. evenly] unevenly Q1.
194. quietness] quickness Q1.
200. That's strange] *om.* Q4–8, F, *which adds* Come, come.
205. bed] Lord Q1.
207. parallel-less] paradise Q1; parrallesse Q2; *see ex. n.*
217. frame] friend Q1.
221. narrow] sparrows' Q1.
225. or] and Q1.
226. way, hid] weighed Q1.
231. disease] deceit Q1.
240. draw] wrack Q1.
244. hate] hate me Q1.
246. Greater for] To Q1.
249. not] *Q1 adds S.D.: He draws his sword.*
265. over of a game] o'er again Q1.
273. S.P. PHILASTER] Q1; *om.* Q2.
283. tender youth] honest looks Q1.
292. mind] frame Q1.
293. hopeless] hapless Q1.
302. for] to Q1.

[III.ii]
3. wak'd, talk'd] make talk Q1.
5. how when] how spoke when Q1.
5. sigh'd, wept, sung] sight song Q1.
8. What, at] What, in Q1; What of Q7; What are Q8, F.
27. I say] *om.* Q3–9, F.
33. my] a Q1.
35. the same] that shame Q1.
37. by my life] by the gods Q1; *see ex. n.*

—137—

Appendix B

46. fair] safe Q4–8, F.
52. cast] mind **Q1**.
53. monuments] mountains **Q1**.
78. Wake] make **Q1**.
81. mourn] warm **Q1**.
90. S.P. PHILASTER] *om.* **Q1**; BELLARIO Q2–9, F.
92. secrecy] service **Q1**.
93. itself] thy sake **Q1**.
105. worthy] wealthy **Q1**.
106. alone] above **Q1**.
109. stern] deep **Q1**.
111. flung] flowing **Q1**.
127. and . . . you] *om.* **Q1**.
146. as pure crystal] *om.* **Q1**.
150. guiltily] vile Q1; guilty Q3–9, F.
159. undergone] undertook **Q1**.
161. men] we **Q1**.
162. men] me **Q1**.
172. grievous] greater **Q1**.
178. Troy] time **Q1**.
180. talk] take **Q1**.

[IV.i]
0.2. *attendants*] *two wood-men* **Q1**.
15. precious] pernicious **Q1**.
16. pursue] pursuit Q4–8, F; *see ex. n.*
16. a] any **Q1**.
31. a man] you **Q1**.
36. dam] damn'd **Q1**.
46. health's sake] Q5–8, F; health sake Q1–4, 9.
48. large] great Q3–9, F.

[IV.ii]
1. deer] *Q1 adds S.D.: Exit King and Lords, Manet Wood-men.*
13. the stewart] his stewart **Q1**.
15. is an] and **Q1**.
17. milking] mitching *Theobald; see ex. n.*

23. fault] or no **Q1**.
32. let's go] else **Q1**.

[IV.iii]
0.1.] *Q1 adds: solus.*
1. these] the **Q1**.
4. women's looks] cruel love **Q1**.
11. at] Out **Q1**.
26 S.P.–31. PHILASTER . . . things] *om.* **Q1**.
42. that way] *Q1 adds: Exit* Philaster
44.1.] *Exit* Boy **Q1**.

[IV.iv]
3. studded] star-dyed Q1; stubbed Q8, F.
18.1 *and attendants*] *om.* Q2–9, F; *and other Lords* **Q1**.
35. thou] then **Q1**.
49. Is . . . heed] Take you heed **Q1**.
55. have] think we have **Q1**.
71. hand] sword **Q1**.
75. spare] leave **Q1**.
75–76. and . . . spawner] here for a spincer **Q1**.

[IV.v]
0.1.] *Q1 adds: solus.*
1. me out a way] out the way **Q1**.
5. S.D. *Sits down*] *om.* Q2–9, F; *She sits down* **Q1**.
18. I am well] *om.* **Q1**.
24. What's] who's **Q1**.
25. here] with his tongue **Q1**.
31. Of . . . down] *om.* Q4–8, F.
31. woman] women Q1, 3, 9.
33. ages in the] *om.* **Q1**.
35. this] my **Q1**.
42. To be enrag'd] to enrage **Q1**.
46. do but] *om.* **Q1**.

—138—

Principal Substantive Variants

52. Thy] Q1; this Q2–9, F.
67. in death] with earth Q1.
69. there] here Q1.
70. then the way] the way to joy Q1.
75.1. Fellow] *Gallant* Q1.
81. good] strong Q1.
81. is able to] would Q1.
89. good fellow] man Q1.
106. loathe] lose Q1.
117. sacred] secret Q1.
122. S.P. DION] OMNES Q1.
124. hurt her] done it Q1.
129. made] let Q1.
133. hand] air Q1.
133. of him] *om.* Q1.
134. to you] *om.* Q1, 4–8, F.
138. fault] sin Q1.
146. go to] *om.* Q1; go F.

[IV.vi]
1. A heaviness near] Oh heavens! heavy Q1.
21. wounds] blood Q1.
24. this sleeping boy] his sleeping body Q1.
24. I ha'] he has Q1.
27. meant] wish'd Q1.
27. pity's sake] pity Q1.
36. Fly, fly] Hide, hide Q1.
38. little] *om.* Q1.
41. good] *om.* Q1.
43. much lov'd] *om.* Q1.
43. breath] *Q1 adds* in't, Shromd [in its shroud].
50. longer] *Q1 adds: Boy falls down.*
51. we have] I Q1.
60. strike] hurt Q3–9, F.
77. suns] Sines Q1.
84. rigor] vigor Q1.
86. that] what Q1.
87. 'Tis the] My Q1.

95. discourse to all] teach Q1.
99. lead me on] bear me hence Q1.
101. do punish] to punish Q1.
113. forth] out Q3–9, F.
114. 'Tis not] Not all Q1.
114. Plutus] *Pluto* Q1.
121. bitter] better Q4–8, F.
126. sure] *Dyce;* sute Q1; say Q2–9, F; *see ex. n.*
129. he will] him well Q1.
135. them] Q1; him Q2–9, F.
142. our] your Q1.
146. To your] With our Q1.
146. match] *Q1 adds: Exit King and* Pharamont.

[V.i]
11. scuffle] shuffle Q1.

[V.ii]
0.1. *in prison*] Q1; *om.* Q2–9, F.
4. shut] Q1; shot Q2–9, F; *see ex. n.*
4. as . . . earth] *om.* Q1.
6. most trusty] truest Q1.
20. by limbs] by time Q1; my limbs Q3–9, F; *see ex. n.*
21. was] liv'd Q1.
24. hours beyond] hour behind Q1.
31. servant] maiden Q1.
33. dear lord] dearest Q1.
34. woman] Q1; women Q2–9, F.
40. Your . . . mine] *Mason;* My . . . yours Q1–9, F; *see ex. n.*
40. price] whit Q1.

[V.iii]
0.1.] *Q1 adds: and a guard.*
6. stay] *Q1 adds S.D.: Exit* Trasiline.
9. be lost] lose it Q1.
9. lightly] slightly Q6–8, F.

—139—

Appendix B

10. overflow] over-throw Q2 *uncor. (Turner, p. 493)*.
11. stack] stock Q1.
14. mightier] weightier Q1.
15. that] the Q1.
17. lays] leaves Q1.
20.1. in . . . garland] *with a garland of flowers on's head* Q1.
23. of these lovers] *om.* Q1.
30. lairs] baits Q2 *uncor. (Turner, p. 493)*.
31. the fervor of] Q1; *om.* Q2–9, F; *see ex. n.*
34. their] that Q1.
37. underbrambles] under branches Q1.
37. divorce] devour Q1.
44. divided] unarm'd Q1.
45. numbers] Q4–8, F; number Q1–3, 9.
47. mighty] worthy Q1.
51. throes] threats Q1.
53. struggled] strangled Q6–8, F.
67. Chaf'd] Q1; Chas'd Q2–5, 9; cast Q6–8, F.
69. Expect] look Q1.
81.] *Q1 adds a line here; see ex. n.*
89. with purest] *om.* Q1.
104. a] my Q4–8, F.
109. Fearing] For Q1.
109. followers] fellows Q1.
113. S.P. 2 MESSENGER] Q1; *Mes.* Q2–9, F.
114. 'em] these Citizens Q1.
116. S.P. 2 MESSENGER] *this edn.; Mes.* Q1–9, F.
123. By my life] by all the gods Q1.
131. shin] skin Q1.
131. have] see Q1.
135. can-carriers] Countrymen Q1.
140. fly] flush Q1.
140. be] ill Q1.

141. murrains reign] injurious rain Q1.
141–142. unbound . . . frieze] in rasine frieze Q1.
150. goatish] goarish Q4–8, F.
154. wild] wide Q1.
154. their] 'your Q1.
155. he] we Q1.
156. they] you Q1.
160. fair] well Q1.
162. countrymen] Citizens Q1.
164–165. and soil you] *om.* Q1.
165. vacation] vocation Q1.
165–166. a brace . . . kicking] and foul shall come up fat And in brave liking Q1.
167. this] that Q1.
170. quench] squench Q8, F.
171. a] Q1, 3–8, F; *om.* Q2.
177. Let . . . it] Let me your goodness know Q1.
185. poor] *om.* Q1.
187. them] her Q1.
189. royal] noble Q1.
190. you] Q1; your Q2–9, F.

V.iv] *See Appendix A for the complete Q1 version of V.iv and V.v.*
1. your] Q1; our Q2–9, F.
4. ope] Q1; up Q2–9, F.
13. darkness] durance Q1.
15. uncut cholers] acute colors Q1.
18. prince] prisoner Q1.
20. hull . . . cockles] stoop to carry coals Q1.
22. what you do] who I am Q1.
29. me] us Q3–9, F.
30. washing] swashing Q3–9, F.
31. see, sweet] huff, sweet Q1; sweet Q3, 9; sweat Q4–7; swear Q8, F.
31. hulk] hock Q1.
35. for] *Weber;* foe Q2–9; Soe F.

—140—

Principal Substantive Variants

74. shin] skin Q3-7.
95. Stuck] struck Q6-8, F.
111. these] those Q4-8, F.
119. make] male [mail] Q8, F.
119. S.D. *strives*] Q7; *strires* Q2; *stirs* Q3-6, 8-9, F.

[V.v]
34. bear] c ear Q8; clear F.
34. her] the Q3-9, F.
47. are] *om.* Q3, 9; be Q4-8, F.
48. heated] hated Q3-9, F.
82. try] Q3-9, F; tire Q2.
178. could I] Q3-9, F; I could Q2.
223. live] Q6-8, F; like Q2-5, 9.

Appendix C

Chronology

Because of their large number and of difficulties in dating, an incomplete list of the "Beaumont and Fletcher" plays is given. Dates are those assigned by E. K. Chambers, *The Elizabethan Stage,* and G. E. Bentley, *The Jacobean and Caroline Stage;* ascriptions of authorship are those of C. H. Hoy, *Studies in Bibliography,* Vols. VIII-XV. Approximate years are indicated by *, occurrences in doubt by (?).

Political and Literary Events   *Life and Works of Beaumont and Fletcher*

1558
Accession of Queen Elizabeth I.
Robert Greene born.
Thomas Kyd born.

1560
George Chapman born.

1561
Francis Bacon born.

1564
Shakespeare born.
Christopher Marlowe born.

1572
Thomas Dekker born.*
John Donne born.*
Massacre of St. Bartholomew's Day.

1573
Ben Jonson born.*

1574
Thomas Heywood born.

1576
The Theatre, the first permanent public theater in London, established by James Burbage.
John Marston born.

CHRONOLOGY

1577
The Curtain theater opened.
Holinshed's *Chronicles of England, Scotland and Ireland.*
Drake begins circumnavigation of the earth; completed 1580.

1578
John Lyly's *Euphues: The Anatomy of Wit.*

1579
Sir Thomas North's translation of Plutarch's Lives.   John Fletcher born at Rye, Sussex.

1580
Thomas Middleton born.

1583
Philip Massinger born.   Sir John Beaumont, brother of Francis, born.

1584   Francis Beaumont born at Grace-Dieu, Leicestershire.*

1586
Death of Sir Philip Sidney.
John Ford born.
Kyd's THE SPANISH TRAGEDY.

1587
The Rose theater opened by Henslowe.
Execution of Mary, Queen of Scots.
Marlowe's TAMBURLAINE, Part I.*
Drake raids Cadiz.

1588
Defeat of the Spanish Armada.
Marlowe's TAMBURLAINE, Part II.*

1589
Marlowe's THE JEW OF MALTA.*
Greene's FRIAR BACON AND FRIAR BUNGAY.*

1590
Spenser's *Faerie Queene* (Books

Appendix C

I–III) published.
Sidney's *Arcadia* published.
Shakespeare's *HENRY VI*, Parts I–III,* *TITUS ANDRONICUS.**

1591
Shakespeare's *RICHARD III.**

Fletcher admitted a pensioner of Bene't (Corpus Christi) College, Cambridge(?).

1592
Marlowe's *DOCTOR FAUSTUS** and *EDWARD II.**
Shakespeare's *TAMING OF THE SHREW** and *THE COMEDY OF ERRORS.**
Death of Greene.

1593
Shakespeare's *LOVES LABOR'S LOST;** *Venus and Adonis* published.
Death of Marlowe.
Theaters closed on account of plague.

1594
Shakespeare's *TWO GENTLEMEN OF VERONA;** *The Rape of Lucrece* published.
Shakespeare's company becomes Lord Chamberlain's Men.
Death of Kyd.

Fletcher takes Cambridge B.A. (?).

1595
The Swan theater built.
Sidney's *Defense of Poesy* published.
Shakespeare's *ROMEO AND JULIET,** *A MIDSUMMER NIGHT'S DREAM,** *RICHARD II.**
Raleigh's first expedition to Guiana.

1596
Spenser's *Faerie Queene* (Books IV–VI) published.
Shakespeare's *MERCHANT OF*

Beaumont matriculates at Broadgates Hall (later Pembroke), Oxford, February 4.

—144—

CHRONOLOGY

VENICE,* KING JOHN.*
James Shirley born.

1597
Bacon's *Essays* (first edition).
Shakespeare's *HENRY IV,* Part I.*

1598
Demolition of The Theatre.
Shakespeare's *MUCH ADO ABOUT NOTHING,* HENRY IV,* Part II.*
Jonson's *EVERY MAN IN HIS HUMOR* (first version).
Seven books of Chapman's translation of Homer's *Iliad* published.

1599
The Paul's Boys reopen their theater.
The Globe theater opened.
Shakespeare's *AS YOU LIKE IT,* HENRY V,* JULIUS CAESAR.**
Marston's *ANTONIO AND MELLIDA,** Parts I and II.
Dekker's *THE SHOEMAKERS' HOLIDAY.**
Death of Spenser.

1600
Shakespeare's *TWELFTH NIGHT.**
The Fortune theater built by Alleyn.
The Children of the Chapel begin to play at the Blackfriars.

1601
Shakespeare's *HAMLET,* MERRY WIVES OF WINDSOR.**
Insurrection and execution of the Earl of Essex.
Jonson's *POETASTER.*

1602
Shakespeare's *TROILUS AND CRESSIDA.**

Fletcher's father, Bishop of London, dies in straitened circumstances.

With brothers John and Henry, Beaumont leaves Oxford upon death of his father.
Fletcher takes Cambridge M.A. (?).

Beaumont enters Inner Temple, November 3.

Beaumont's first verse published—a commendatory poem prefixed

Appendix C

to Sir John Beaumont's *Metamorphosis of Tobacco*. Followed by *Salmacis and Hermaphroditus*.

1603
Death of Queen Elizabeth I; accession of James VI of Scotland as James I.
Florio's translation of Montaigne's *Essays* published.
Shakespeare's *ALL'S WELL THAT ENDS WELL.*
Heywood's *A WOMAN KILLED WITH KINDNESS.*
Marston's *THE MALCONTENT.**
Shakespeare's company becomes the King's Men.

1604
Shakespeare's *MEASURE FOR MEASURE,* *OTHELLO.**
Marston's *THE FAWN.**
Chapman's *BUSSY D'AMBOIS.**

1605
Shakespeare's *KING LEAR.**
Marston's *THE DUTCH COURTESAN.**
Bacon's *Advancement of Learning* published.
The Gunpowder Plot.

Beaumont comes into an inheritance upon death of elder brother, Sir Henry.
Fletcher's *WOMAN'S PRIZE.**

1606
Shakespeare's *MACBETH.**
Jonson's *VOLPONE.**
Tourneur's *REVENGER'S TRAGEDY.**
The Red Bull theater built.
Death of John Lyly.

Beaumont's *THE WOMAN HATER.**

1607
Shakespeare's *ANTONY AND CLEOPATRA.**
Settlement of Jamestown, Virginia.

Beaumont's *KNIGHT OF THE BURNING PESTLE.**
Jonson's *VOLPONE*, with commendatory verses by Fletcher and Beaumont, published.
Beaumont and Fletcher collabora-

CHRONOLOGY

1608
Shakespeare's *CORIOLANUS*,* *TIMON OF ATHENS*,* *PERICLES*.*
Chapman's *CONSIPRACY AND TRAGEDY OF CHARLES, DUKE OF BYRON*.*
Richard Burbage leases Blackfriars theater for King's company.
John Milton born.

1609
Shakespeare's *CYMBELINE*;* *Sonnets* published.
Jonson's *EPICOENE*.
Dekker's *Gull's Hornbook* published.

1610
Jonson's *ALCHEMIST*.
Chapman's *REVENGE OF BUSSY D'AMBOIS*.*
Richard Crashaw born.

1611
Authorized (King James) Version of the Bible published.
Shakespeare's *THE WINTER'S TALE*,* *THE TEMPEST*.*
Middleton's *A CHASTE MAID IN CHEAPSIDE*.
Tourneur's *ATHEIST'S TRAGEDY*.*
Chapman's translation of *Iliad* completed.

1612
Webster's *THE WHITE DEVIL*.*

tion begins.*
Beaumont's *THE WOMAN HATER*, with revisions by Fletcher, published.

Fletcher's *FAITHFUL SHEPHERDESS*.*

Beaumont and Fletcher's *PHILASTER*,* *COXCOMB*.* They affiliate with the King's Men.*

Beaumont and Fletcher's *CAPTAIN*,* *MAID'S TRAGEDY*.*

Jonson's CATILINE, with commendatory verses by Fletcher and Beaumont, published.
Beaumont and Fletcher's *A KING AND NO KING*.

Beaumont's epistle to Elizabeth, Countess of Rutland. He writes commendatory verses to Jonson's *EPICOENE*, first printed in the Jonson Folio of 1616.*

—147—

Appendix C

	Fletcher and Shakespeare's *CARDENIO* (?).*
	Fletcher marries Joan Herring (?).
1613	
The Globe theater burned.	Beaumont's *INNER TEMPLE MASQUE.*
Webster's *THE DUCHESS OF MALFI.*	Beaumont marries Ursula Isley; collaboration with Fletcher ends.*
Sir Thomas Overbury murdered.	Fletcher and Shakespeare's *TWO NOBLE KINSMEN, HENRY VIII* *
	Fletcher, Field, and Massinger's *HONEST MAN'S FORTUNE.*
1614	
The Globe theater rebuilt.	Fletcher's *WIT WITHOUT MONEY* * (later revised?).
The Hope theater built.	
Jonson's *BARTHOLOMEW FAIR.*	
1616	
Publication of Folio edition of Jonson's *Works.*	Beaumont and Fletcher's *THE SCORNFUL LADY* published
Chapman's *Whole Works of Homer.*	Fletcher's *MAD LOVER.* *
Death of Shakespeare.	Death of Beaumont, March 6.
1617	
	Fletcher's *CHANCES.* *
1618	
Outbreak of Thirty Years War.	Fletcher's *LOYAL SUBJECT.*
Execution of Raleigh.	
1619	
	THE MAID'S TRAGEDY and *A KING AND NO KING* published.
	Fletcher and Massinger's *SIR JOHN VAN OLDEN BARNAVELT.*
	Fletcher's *HUMOROUS LIEUTENANT.*
1620	
Settlement of Plymouth, Massachusetts.	*PHILASTER* published.
	Fletcher and Massinger's *CUSTOM OF THE COUNTRY,* * *FALSE ONE.* *

CHRONOLOGY

1621
Middleton's *WOMEN BEWARE WOMEN.**

Robert Burton's *Anatomy of Melancholy* published.
Andrew Marvell born.

1622
Middleton and Rowley's *THE CHANGELING.**
Henry Vaughan born.

1623
Publication of Folio edition of Shakespeare's *COMEDIES, HISTORIES, AND TRAGEDIES.*

1624

1625
Death of King James I; accession of Charles I.

1626
Death of Bacon.
Death of Tourneur.

1627
Death of Middleton.

1628
Ford's *THE LOVER'S MELANCHOLY.*
Petition of Right.
Buckingham assassinated.

1631
Shirley's *THE TRAITOR.*
Death of Donne.
John Dryden born.

1632
Massinger's *THE CITY MADAM.**

Beaumont, Fletcher, and Massinger's *THIERRY AND THEODORET* published.
Fletcher and Massinger's *DOUBLE MARRIAGE.**
Fletcher's *PILGRIM** and *WILD GOOSE CHASE.**

Fletcher and Massinger's *PROPHETESS, SPANISH CURATE, SEA VOYAGE.*

Fletcher and Massinger's *LITTLE FRENCH LAWYER.**
Fletcher and Rowley's *MAID IN THE MILL.*

Fletcher's *RULE A WIFE AND HAVE A WIFE, WIFE FOR A MONTH.*

Fletcher's *FAIR MAID OF THE INN* (with Massinger, Webster and Ford).
Death of Fletcher.

—149—

Appendix C

1633
Donne's *Poems* published.
Death of George Herbert.

1634
Death of Chapman, Marston, Webster.*
Milton's *Comus*.

Publication of *THE TWO NOBLE KINSMEN*, with title-page attribution to Shakespeare and Fletcher.

1635
Sir Thomas Browne's *Religio Medici*.

1637
Death of Jonson.

THE ELDER BROTHER published.

1639
First Bishops' War.
Death of Carew.*

MONSIEUR THOMAS, WIT WITHOUT MONEY, ROLLO DUKE OF NOMANDY published.

1640
Short Parliament.
Long Parliament impeaches Laud.
Death of Massinger, Burton.

THE NIGHT WALKER, THE CORONATION published.

1641
Irish rebel.
Death of Heywood.

1642
Charles I leaves London; Civil War breaks out.
Shirley's *COURT SECRET*.
All theaters closed by Act of Parliament.

1643
Parliament swears to the Solemn League and Covenant.

1645
Ordinance for New Model Army enacted.

1646
End of First Civil War.

1647
Army occupies London.

First Folio edition of Beaumont

Charles I forms alliance with Scots.

1648
Second Civil War.

1649
Execution of Charles I.

1650
Jeremy Collier born.

1651
Hobbes' *Leviathan* published.

1652
First Dutch War begins (ended 1654).
Thomas Otway born.

1653
Nathaniel Lee born.*

1656
D'Avenant's THE SIEGE OF RHODES performed at Rutland House.

1657
John Dennis born.

1658
Death of Oliver Cromwell
D'Avenant's THE CRUELTY OF THE SPANIARDS IN PERU performed at the Cockpit.

1660
Restoration of Charles II.
Treatrical patents granted to Thomas Killigrew and Sir William D'Avenant, authorizing them to form, respectively, the King's and the Duke of York's Companies.

1661
Cowley's THE CUTTER OF COLEMAN STREET.
D'Avenant's THE SIEGE OF RHODES (expanded to two parts).
and Fletcher's COMEDIES AND TRAGEDIES published.

Appendix C

1662
Charter granted to the Royal Society.

1663
Dryden's *THE WILD GALLANT*.
Tuke's *THE ADVENTURES OF FIVE HOURS*.

1664
Sir John Vanbrugh born.
Dryden's *THE RIVAL LADIES*.
Dryden and Howard's *THE INDIAN QUEEN*.
Etherege's *THE COMICAL REVENGE*.

1665
Second Dutch War begins (ended 1667).
Great Plague.
Dryden's *THE INDIAN EMPEROR*.
Orrery's *MUSTAPHA*.

1666
Fire of London.
Death of James Shirley.

DATE DUE